P U B W A
― I N ―
Suffolk

THIRTY CIRCULAR WALKS
AROUND SUFFOLK INNS

Jean and Geoff Pratt

COUNTRYSIDE BOOKS
NEWBURY, BERKSHIRE

COUNTRYSIDE BOOKS
3 Catherine Road
Newbury, Berkshire

ISBN 1 85306 287 1

Designed by Mon Mohan
Cover illustration by Colin Doggett
Photographs and maps by the authors

Produced through MRM Associates Ltd., Reading
Typeset by Paragon Typesetters, Queensferry, Clwyd
Printed in England

Contents

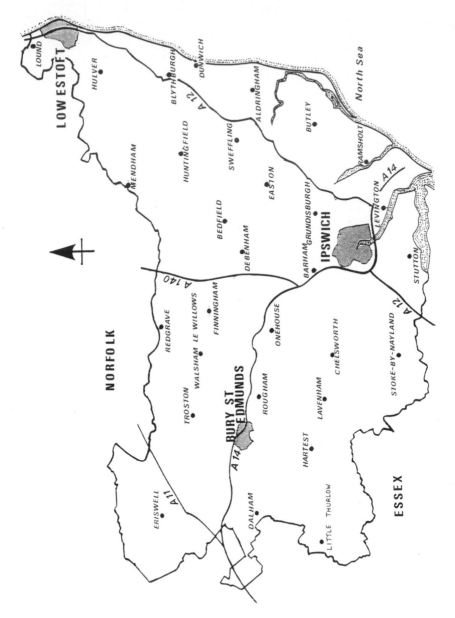

Area map showing locations of the walks.

Publisher's Note

We hope that you obtain considerable enjoyment from this book; great care has been taken in its preparation. However, changes of landlord and actual closures are sadly not uncommon. Likewise, although at the time of publication all routes followed public rights of way or well-established permitted paths, diversion orders can be made and permissions withdrawn.

We cannot accept responsibility for any inaccuracies, but we are anxious that all details covering both pubs and walks are kept up to date, and would therefore welcome information from readers which would be relevant to future editions.

Introduction

Suffolk is endowed with a rich variety of landscapes, arising mainly from the different types of soil which occur in the county and the pattern of rivers and streams draining the area. The Sandlings is an area of light sand between the coast from Felixstowe to Lowestoft and the line of the A12 road. Here sandy fields, dependent upon irrigation for successful crops, are interspersed with wild, rough heathland and forests. High Suffolk, an area of clay, forms the rich arable heart of the county. The Brecklands, in the north-west, is a plateau of very light sand overlaying chalk, where wide fields bordered by Scots pine shelter belts are seen and where there are large tracts of forest. Many rivers carve their way out to beautiful estuaries or to the coast, their river valleys forming excellent walking areas.

The areas for these 30 walks were selected to give a good geographical spread over Suffolk. The pubs were chosen for their good ale and food, as well as for their attractive location and friendly atmosphere. Another consideration, in each case, was that there should be a network of public footpaths in the vicinity, providing a pleasant, fairly easy walk from the pub.

Inns today are as much restaurants as a venue for beer drinking. All but one of these serve food – excellent, interesting meals. More and more now make provision for the entertainment of children, so that a visit to the pub can be a family occasion. One enterprising establishment has a children's garden bar in summer, serving Coke and lemonade.

The majority of the pubs in this book are open from 11 am till about 2.30 pm and again from about 6 pm till 11 pm on weekdays. Invariably, on Sundays they are open from 12 noon till 3 pm and from 7 pm till 10.30 pm. Significant variations are mentioned in the text. Times may vary with the season. Meals are, in general, served from 12 noon till 2 pm and from 7 pm till 9.30 pm. Some pubs have one evening or day each week when they do not serve meals, and some only serve lunches. These facts are also mentioned. Telephone numbers are given so that you may check on opening hours; do phone if timing is crucial.

To comply with food hygiene laws, dogs are not usually allowed in the restaurant, and before taking them in the bar area, on a lead, the landlord's advice should be sought.

Even in dry East Anglia it can rain occasionally, so have thought for the weather and rainwear. Stout walking shoes or boots are a sensible choice.

Most landlords are happy for you to leave your vehicle in the pub car park while out walking, in the expectation of a hungry, thirsty walker coming in later. However it is reasonable to ask first, as a car left unaccounted for in the car park can be a worry these days. When available, suitable public car parks are mentioned, though in many villages the pub has the only car park. It is often possible to park on a verge or at the roadside in or near a village, but care must be taken to avoid causing an obstruction or damaging a verge.

The appropriate Ordnance Survey Landranger map is listed for each walk. These show by red dotted lines the public rights of way. The sketch maps in the book, which are not to scale, are intended to supplement the Ordnance Survey sheets. At the time of going to press, the A45 trunk road through Suffolk and Cambridgeshire is about to be renumbered as the A14 and this reference number has been used throughout this book. Readers may, however, find references to the old number on maps and elsewhere.

Finally, we hope that this series of walks throughout Suffolk will be enjoyed by those who use this book, and that they will be further encouraged to explore and get to know more of the county's varied countryside.

Jean and Geoff Pratt

Little Thurlow
The Cock

Little Thurlow, near the south-west corner of the county, is a charming village with many thatched cottages. At one time Sir Stephen Soame, Lord Mayor of London, lived at Little Thurlow Hall and entertained King Charles II there. He built the almshouses on the hill on the Little Bradley to Little Thurlow road, and the schoolhouse, in 1614, at the junction in the village. There are similar crests above the doors. Although only 4 miles from its source the river Stour has already gained a lot of water – it is no mean river. After leaving Little Thurlow the Stour forms the border between Suffolk and Essex for most of the way to the broad estuary at Cattawade and on to the sea at Harwich and Shotley.

The Cock was built in 1614 and was a coaching inn on the Newmarket to Colchester route. It is a large but quiet pub, with two wide old fireplaces in the long bar which runs the full width of the building. The pub does not serve meals, so walkers who bring their sandwiches are welcomed. Behind the pub is a garden for summer drinking and for children's play. Well-mannered dogs are welcome. Greene King ales are served.

Telephone: 044 083 224.

How to get there: The Thurlows, Great and Little, are about 4 miles north of Haverhill and on the B1061, which runs between Newmarket and the A143 at Little Wratting. The Cock is in the centre of Little Thurlow.

Parking: There is a car park at the rear of the pub.

Length of the walk: 2½ miles. Map: OS Landranger 154 Cambridge and Newmarket (GR 678508).

This pleasant walk crosses the river Stour twice and visits the village of Little Bradley. The area is gently undulating, which gives good views over this rural scene. Much of the walk is on firm farm tracks, some very minor roads and some good cross-field paths.

The Walk

From the pub, turn right along the main street for 80 yards, and after the white thatched house turn left towards Culyers, on a surfaced track, with a brick wall on the right and a paling fence on the left. The tarmac ends by the house on the right, but keep straight on along a cart track. Pass a three-step stile on the right and, when the track ends, go through the wooden farm gate into light woodland, and in 50 yards go over an attractive newish bridge over the Stour and turn left.

Follow the wide track, with woodland on the right. Presently the track curves round to the right, climbing up to the edge of a large field. Go left along the field edge, with trees on the left, to the corner.

At the corner, near a small brick building, go right for about 150 yards, then left, to walk out to a concrete track. Follow this all the way out to a road. As you go, see Little Thurlow church down on your left in the trees. Turn right on this road with wide grass verges, called, appropriately, Broad Road, and climb up through the hamlet of Little Thurlow Green. Pass a thatched cottage called The Old Inn, and go on, past a widening verge on the right where a telephone box and a dark pink cottage stand.

Keep on the quiet road to the crest of the hill, past Green Farm Barn, on round the bend to the left and downhill again till the road swings right. Here, by a cross-hedge on the left, leave the road and walk along a headland path, with a hedge on the right. In 100 yards follow the hedge as it goes right and continue till you reach a wooden farm gate by the corner of a shelter belt. Pass through the gate and head across the meadow towards Hall Farm. Go through the metal gate and up the concrete ramp, on across the farmyard, between farm buildings and along the concrete track, with Little Bradley church away to your left, up to join a road.

9

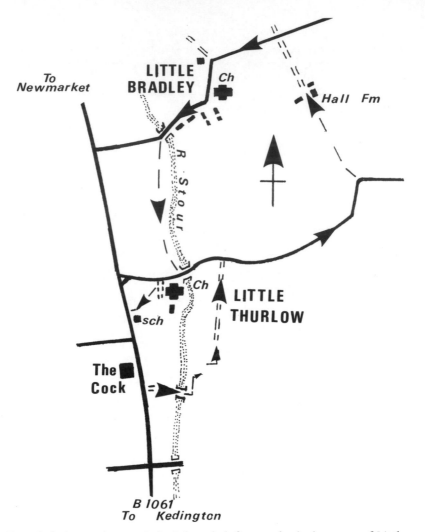

To Newmarket

LITTLE BRADLEY

Ch

Hall Fm

R. Stour

Ch

LITTLE THURLOW

sch

The Cock

B 1061
To Kedington

Turn left down the road. As it bends left pass the lodge gate of Little Bradley House, and so reach All Saints church. John Daye, a printer, who died in 1584, is commemorated in a 19th century stained-glass window here. John Foxe lodged with John Daye, and the latter printed the first English edition of Foxe's Book of Martyrs. He was also one of the first to print music.

After the church the road crosses a bridge. Go right into Little Bradley. Pass the broad green on your left, with a large black barn in the middle, Maltings Farmhouse, and on over a brick bridge across the river Stour.

10

Turn half-left across a large field. The path is well defined, and heads directly towards the church at Little Thurlow. At the corner of the field, pass between the river and the small cemetery to reach a road. Cross straight over and go up the path to St Peter's church. The canopied tomb of Sir Stephen Soame is inside.

Leave the churchyard at the west end, go right a little on the gravel track and, by a wooden farm gate quite close to the road, take a path which goes diagonally across a field, between fences. Look back over your left shoulder to see an attractive 2½-storey, apricot-washed cottage, with on its right an old timbered barn with brick-nogging. At the far end of this field, cross a concrete footbridge and go through a gate into a meadow.

Head for the right of the school on the far side, and there, near a white farm gate, go through a kissing-gate into a short lane which leads out to the road. Turn left, go over the bridge, past the old schoolhouse at the road junction, and back to the Cock inn.

2 Eriswell
The Chequers

Eriswell is on the edge of the Brecklands at the north-west corner of the county, not far from a big air base. On a few houses passed on this walk you will see the letters NEC. They stand for 'New England Company'. Before the Civil War many of the local estates were owned by the Bedingfield family. When the war began the Bedingfields were on the side of King Charles I and their loyalty to him led to Oliver Cromwell taking their estates from them. Meanwhile the Puritans had heard of, and disapproved of, the heathen ways of the North American Indians. A vast amount of money in those days, £12,000, was raised nationally, to send out missionaries to educate the North American Indians and teach them about Christianity. The money was used to buy the Eriswell estates, and the revenue from the estates was invested in the New England Company, for the propagation of the Gospel in New England and for the education of North American Indians. The company existed for over 200 years. In 1818 the New England Company funds were used to bring one North American Indian lad, called James Paul, over to Eriswell to be educated and to learn the trade of a carpenter and builder, but in November two years later he died, aged 16, and is buried in Eriswell churchyard. In 1869 the

Charity Commissioners sold the NEC's Eriswell lands to the deposed ruler of the Punjab, Maharajah Duleep Singh. In 1894 the lands were once more sold, this time to Lord Iveagh.

The Chequers inn is 200 years old, and although it has recently been extensively modernised, it remains a very friendly pub, with an excellent reputation for good food. The speciality is authentic Mexican food and customers come from miles around to enjoy the hot, spicy dishes. Nachos grandes, chicken fajitas, tex mex enchiladas, and country chilli beef casserole with chips or baked potatoes are among the many dishes on offer. More traditional dishes served are lemon sole with crabmeat filling, garlic breaded chicken goujons, cottage pie, lasagne and macaroni cheese. Real ales on offer include Greene King IPA and Abbot. Dry Blackthorn cider is also available. Children are welcome and dogs are allowed in the garden area.

Telephone: 0638 532478.

How to get there: Eriswell is 2 miles north of Mildenhall. It is reached from the A1065 Brandon road. The Chequers is in the village, just beyond the church.

Parking: There is plenty of parking behind the Chequers.

Length of the walk: Almost 4 miles. Map: OS Landranger 143 Ely and Wisbech (GR 723782).

This is a fairly easy walk near the border of Suffolk and where the sandy Brecks meet the flat fenland of Cambridgeshire. After a grassy path through farmland, the walk crosses, and follows for a short distance, the Cut-Off Channel. It continues along a leafy forest trail to the edge of Mildenhall. The return is along a green lane and across fields and back over the channel.

The Walk

From the Chequers go left along the road, passing the church of St Laurence and St Peter. Go straight ahead along the grassy track between the former rectory and the nursery school. Follow it between fields, and on, curving to the right and then to the left. Take a rest on the bench under a tree by a bend in the green lane. Later you will be walking along an avenue of Scots pines.

Turn right at a T-junction of paths and go over the concrete bridge over the Cut-Off Channel. This bridge is over the top of a sluice, as you can see by the difference in water levels. There is a gauge fixed to the side. This is part of a drainage channel, a 28-mile canal constructed in the 1950s. It intercepts flood water from the river Lark near Barton Mills, and conveys the water direct to the Great Ouse at

13

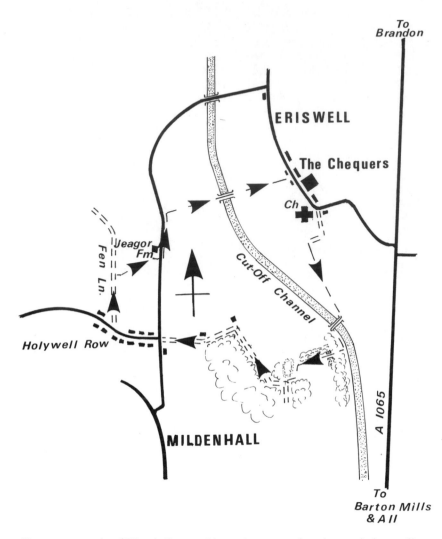

To
Brandon

ERISWELL

The Chequers

Ch

Cut-Off Channel

Ueagor Fm

Fen Ln.

Holywell Row

MILDENHALL

A 1065

To
Barton Mills
& A11

Denver, south of King's Lynn. Along its route the channel also collects
water from the upper reaches of the rivers Little Ouse and Wissey.

After the bridge turn left along the grassy track beside the channel.
In 200 yards look out for a narrow footpath off right, with an ash on
its right and a sycamore on its left, going steeply up a sandy bank for
15 yards. Go up there. No sooner are you at the open top of this bank
than you descend again steeply into woods. Cross another bridge and
carry on.

14

Just after crossing a stream, you come to the corner of a field surrounded by trees, silver birches to the left, Scots pines to the right. Follow the line of pines on your right. At the corner of this field, leave the track you have been on and turn left beside a ditch on the right. In a little under 100 yards go right to cross the shallow ditch and continue in roughly the same direction for a few yards.

The path swings right, gets wider and you reach an area with mature trees, with a cart track leading to the left by a Forestry Commission notice. Join the track going straight on, along a grassy track near the edge of the woodland among Scots pines, a few oaks and bracken, with a field seen on your right. By a cream-washed chalet-bungalow your track swings left, and in 50 more yards you join an earth track, with woodland on the left still. Pass a junction off right to Gamekeepers Cottage. Later pass a farm and a few houses and reach a crossroads.

Go straight over, along the road opposite, for ¼ mile. Near a bend to the right, between Green Leys and The Orchards, turn right along a byway. Follow Fen Lane, this broad, sandy track, for roughly 300 yards until you come to a cross-track. Take the path on the right, going over a stile which is set back from the track, into the corner of a rather rough field. Go diagonally across this field towards the right of all the farm buildings and join a road by a stile.

Cross straight over the road into the field and turn left, walking inside the field, but parallel to the road on your left, as far as the corner. Turn right and walk with the hedge on the left. At a cross-ditch go down two steps and over the footbridge. At the field end go over a wooden stile on to a footbridge over the Cut-Off Channel.

Keep straight on towards the village, seen half-right, with a barbed wire fence on the left. Cross a farm track, go through a gap and then between two rows of trees. Another gap takes you beside garages out to the road. Turn right and walk back to the Chequers.

Dalham
The Affleck Arms

Dalham is in the far west of the county. The small village itself lies in the valley of the river Kennett, though the church and Dalham Hall are on the hill slopes to the north-east. In picturesque Dalham, four out of five houses have a thatched roof. Memorials to the Affleck family abound in the church and churchyard, some dating back to 1718. The consideration of the landowners for their loyal servants is seen in the kindly memorials on the outside of the north and east church walls.

The thatched Affleck Arms, which fronts the little river and the main road, is Elizabethan. The pub is open both at lunchtimes and in the evenings for meals, seven days a week. Typical of the fare are home-made steak and kidney pie, seafood platter, omelettes, grilled cod or plaice, and treacle and walnut tart. Traditional Sunday roasts are served. The real ales are Greene King IPA and Abbot, and Dry Blackthorn draught cider is available. In winter a cheerful log fire burns. For children there is a family room, a play area outside and, in summer, a pets' corner. Dogs are best left in the car, or tethered in the yard.

Telephone: 0638 500306.

16

How to get there: From Newmarket, 5 miles to the west of Dalham, take the B1063 road to Ashley and then keep straight on for 2 miles. Coming from the east, use the A14 dual carriageway and take the turn to Newmarket (B1506). Shortly after leaving the A14, take a left turn to Gazeley and, after passing Gazeley church, fork left to reach Dalham in 1½ miles. The Affleck Arms is in the centre of the village, beside the river Kennett.

Parking: There is a large car park at the rear of the Affleck Arms. The access is from the road to Ashley.

Length of the walk: 4½ miles. Map: OS Landranger 154 Cambridge and Newmarket, 155 Bury St Edmunds and Sudbury (GR 722617).

This easy ramble on the side of the Kennett valley passes Dalham church, with its memorial to Cecil Rhodes, and follows the Icknield Way across the parkland and woods surrounding Dalham Hall, to a ridge with good views to the north, and thence to the village of Gazeley. The return route is down to the river Kennett and back along the river bank.

The Icknield Way is a regional long-distance route from Ivinghoe Beacon in Buckinghamshire to Knettishall Heath in Suffolk. It follows, as far as is now possible or convenient, an ancient trackway which once, linked with the Ridgeway in the west and Peddars Way in the east, formed a major route across Britain. An ancient M4 perhaps?

The Walk

From the Affleck Arms take the road towards Gazeley, beside the river Kennett. Having left the river bank, the road passes, on the left, the remains of a disused malt kiln. Very soon after, turn right, off the road along a footpath flanked by chestnut trees. Note the unusual sign erected by the parish about keeping to the 4 ft wide footpath. The avenue of chestnuts which you are following is repeated by a similar avenue 100 yards to the left. These trees flank a broad vista to Dalham Hall. The footpath, which forms part of the Icknield Way, leads to Dalham church. In the corner of the churchyard nearest to Dalham Hall is a memorial to Cecil Rhodes, a builder of the British Empire and founder of the former African state of Rhodesia, now Zimbabwe. In 1900 he bought the hall and 3,000 acres of land here. His brothers and sisters lie buried in the churchyard. With much of his great wealth, gained from gold and diamond mining, he endowed Rhodes Scholarships at Oxford. The handsome church once had a spire soaring 40 ft above the present tower. In a great storm in 1658, on the day on which Oliver Cromwell died, the spire blew down.

At the church, turn right on a narrow tarmac road but, where it

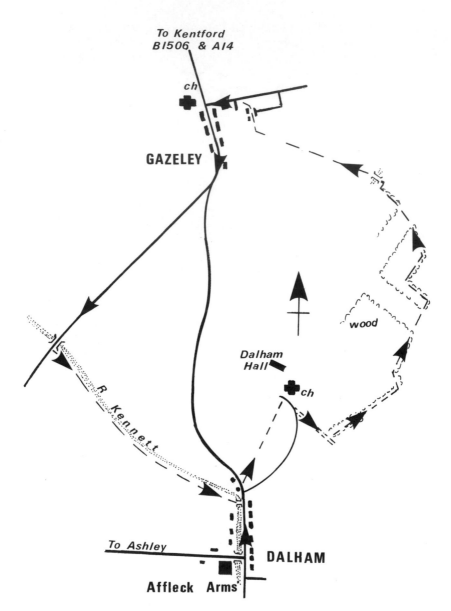

bears right, keep straight on with woods on the right and parkland on the left. In about 200 yards, where the field on the left ends by some iron railings, turn left on a grassy footpath through a wooded shelter

18

belt. The path comes out into a large field. Continue in the same direction, following the edge of the tree belt on your left. When you reach the corner of the field, turn sharp left and enter the trees, keeping parallel to the edge of the wood, a few yards away to the right. In about ¼ mile leave Brick Kiln Wood, but keep straight on with a hedge on the right and a long narrow meadow stretching away to the left.

In about 100 yards enter Blocksey Wood and here again keep within the wood, but a few yards from the edge. The path turns left, right, left and right again before you come out alongside another long meadow to the left. Cross the head of this field, which is part of the parkland surrounding Dalham Hall, and at the corner the path enters Bluebutton Wood. Still follow the edge of the wood. The path makes a sharp right turn and you reach the edge of a field. Turn left and in a few yards, at the corner, cross a bridge and enter another field. Go straight on, with the hedge on the left.

At the field boundary continue on a wide grassy track, following a line of wooden electricity poles. Go through a gap in a cross-hedge beside a large electricity pole and then straight across an arable field into a narrow tarmac path, between brick garden walls, which leads to the head of a cul-de-sac.

Cross the end of the cul-de-sac, turn left beside the corner of No 22 and go out to the road by the '40' sign. Follow the road left, for about 200 yards, to a T-junction by All Saints church, Gazeley. Here, leave the Icknield Way path and turn left. Walk down the village street and in nearly ½ mile, at the fork in the road, bear right. Keep downhill on the road for about ¾ mile, with fine views to the left and right. At the bottom, cross the bridge with steel railings over the river Kennett and in 50 yards turn left through a narrow belt of woodlands and rejoin the Icknield Way.

Follow the wide grassy riverside path which leads, in almost a mile, to a stile and thence to a wooden footbridge over the river Kennett, to reach the road in Dalham. Turn right, back to the Affleck Arms.

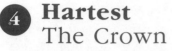# Hartest
The Crown

Deep in rural south-west Suffolk, Hartest nestles beside a stream at the junction of four valleys. It is surrounded by hills, all about 100 ft above the village. It is a very compact place. Buildings cluster around the attractive triangular green, near a corner of which stands All Saints church with its tower of diapered work in brick and flint. There is a large boulder on the green – possibly an erratic from an early ice age. Similar isolated stones appear in a few places in the county.

Next door to the church is the Crown inn, which was once a 16th century manor house. The inn, though large, is subdivided into several separate areas. There is the restaurant, the lounge bar with its roaring wood fire and another dining area in what was the old court room in days long gone. The wrought-iron bar rail is somewhat unusual, as is the collection of keys.

This Greene King pub serves a varied menu, but specialises in fish dishes, for example, fresh Dover sole grilled in butter, fresh fillet of plaice, and grilled Scotch salmon in a prawn and lobster sauce. Meat dishes include grilled Scotch sirloin steak, gammon steak and pineapple, and breast of chicken in a white wine and mushroom sauce. During the winter the inn has speciality all-in menus every

Monday evening and fresh mussels every Friday evening. The real ales served are IPA and Abbot. Draught cider, Blackthorn Dry, is available.
Telephone: 0284 830250.

How to get there: Hartest is 8 miles north of Sudbury. It lies on the B1066, which runs between the A1092 at a point ½ mile west of Long Melford (A134) and Bury. The Crown is at the south side of the green, close to the church.

Parking: There is plenty of parking at the Crown.

Length of the walk: 5 miles. Map: OS Landranger 155 Bury St Edmunds and Sudbury (GR 834524).

The walk, which is fairly easy, circles the village, keeping largely to the high land, with fine views over Hartest. Although the whole walk is 5 miles long there are ample opportunities to take short-cuts back to the start, as the route crosses the five roads which radiate from the village green.

The Walk

From the green by the Crown, go towards the church, and through a gap in a low brick wall, to a path between the inn and the drive to the rectory. (It can also be reached directly from the edge of the car park.) At first there is an iron fence on the left, later the brick wall of the rectory. Go over a wooden footbridge and climb quite steeply up the rough hill, cross a footbridge and enter a very big field. Turn left and continue climbing steadily up the left edge of the field.

Stop now and again to look down on this picture book village. Below is the church, next to it is the three-storey, grey, slate-roofed rectory, thatched cottages, cottages with dormer windows, cottages with mansard roofs, and there, in the centre, is the green.

At the top corner of the field go through a thickish cross-hedge and continue at the edge of the field with a steep bank below on your left. The field edge bends round to the right – keep with it, climbing, until you reach a bank ahead, which leads even more steeply up to a field.

Go left, still rising, with that bank on your right and walk out to the road by white, thatched Pippin Cottage. Turn left along the road, and after the chalet bungalow, Larkrise, turn right along a cart track, with a hedge on the right at first, later just a ditch and bank on the right. At the field end there is a locked metal gate with a gap beside it. Go through, and on, diagonally across the field, heading a bit left of the slender tower in the distance, with Lord's Farm on your right. The path reaches a concrete farm drive by a sort of squeezer stile, cunningly contrived to keep horses, but not humans, out.

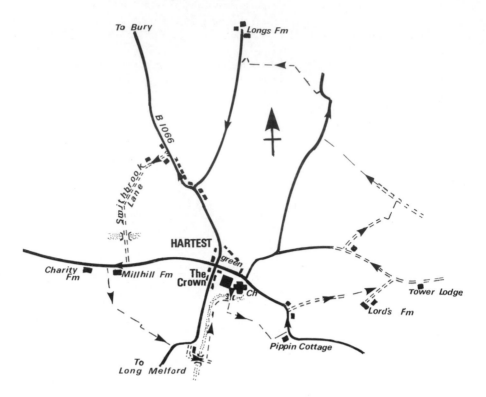

Turn left along the farm track. At the T-junction, with Tower Cottage ahead, go left down the concrete track. In about 400 yards, just after a house on the right, turn right at the side of the house, and then in a few yards take the path that leads straight on between the hedge on the left and the bank on the right, climbing steadily. Near the crest of the hill is a cross-hedge on the left. Go just beyond it and turn left, to have that hedge on your left.

Continue to the end, where you meet a cinder track and turn left. In 100 yards the track divides. Carry straight on until it curves left a little. There is a shallow ditch and a hedge on the left. Go through a cross-hedge by a gap. Continue along the left edge of the next field, with the hedge on the left. At the end of this field, leave it by a culvert over a deep ditch and enter a big, L-shaped field. Walk out across the field for 100 yards to the Lawshall road. Turn right. The road curves left and then right. As it starts to go right, by a prominent ash tree, peel off the road to the left, and in 10 yards bear round to the right, keeping the hedge on your right. When that hedge ends, by a culvert into a field on your right, turn left and head along a path to the right of a tall oak, towards a smaller oak and other trees.

From that clump of trees, at a field corner, carry on down the hill quite steeply, with a hedge on the left, on a farm track. At the bottom of the field, go right for 50 yards, then left and walk out to the road. On your right up the farm drive is Longs Farm.

Turn left and walk up past Vallance Farm, then on down past Tan Office Farm to meet a road at Cross Green, where the pink-washed house at the junction has lachrymose barge boards. Turn right and go up the road with houses on the right. After passing woods on the right, you come to a large creamish-coloured house on the left. Immediately after that, turn left down a gravel cart track. In 200 yards pass a bungalow, Little Croft, and bear slightly left along the lane with a hedge and a ditch on the left. The lane leads steeply down into a valley, where it crosses a bridge over a watercourse, and goes straight up the other side. Join a road at right angles, turn right and almost immediately pass, on the left, Millhill Farmhouse with its pargeted plaster walls. Observe 200 yards ahead the white, thatched Charity Farm.

Go on the road halfway to the Charity Farm boundary, then turn left and cross the field to the opposite hedge, where you will find a waymarked gap. Go through and follow a hedge on the left. At the field corner go left, with the hedge on the right. You are now looking down on another valley, and across the other side you can see white Pippin Cottage, where you were earlier in the walk.

Soon you come to a wide gap in the hedge on the right. Follow the waymarks through the gap, to continue walking with the hedge on the left out to a road at a bend. Bear slightly left and go downhill on the road. At the bottom, where the road bends left, go right alongside a terrace of houses. Beyond the buildings turn left, over a stream by a brick parapeted bridge, on a track which leads to Brick House Farm. In 15 yards turn left off the track to follow the fast flowing stream, which is on the left, at the bottom of a steep high bank. Pass a bridge leading to bungalows, then follow the stream round to the right to reach the substantial bridge, leading to the church and pub, which you used at the start. Cross the bridge and return to the Crown.

Troston
The Bull

Troston is about 5 miles south of the Norfolk border, and is on the southern edge of that part of East Anglia known as the Brecklands, an area of light sandy soils.

The Bull, built in the 17th century, has a warm friendly atmosphere. It offers accommodation and it serves delicious food. You can have pâté on toast, prawn cocktail or melon balls in port, tagliatelle, chilli con carne, moussaka, lemon sole with crabmeat, a 20 oz T-bone steak or a range of vegetarian dishes. Sweets include banana split, home-made apple pie or bread-and-butter pudding with butterscotch sauce. A choice of three roasts is offered on Sundays. Meals are served daily from 12 noon till 2 pm, and, on every day except Sunday, from 7 pm till 9 pm. Greene King brews are the order of the day. Dry Blackthorn draught cider is also available. There is a garden for the children to play in, and children dining with their parents are welcome inside. Dogs, however, are not permitted in the pub.

Telephone: 0359 269358.

How to get there: Troston is 1½ miles west of the A1088, the Stowmarket to Thetford road, near Ixworth. Close to the northern

24

end of the Ixworth bypass there is a small turning, signed 'Troston'. The Bull is at the T-junction in the centre of the village.

Parking: The pub has a large car park at the side.

Length of the walk: 5½ miles. Map: OS Landranger 144 Thetford and Breckland (GR 898722).

One of the many delights of this walk is to come out of the trees and suddenly to be confronted by the big stretch of water known as Ampton Water. The walk crosses it by surely one of the longest footbridges in Suffolk.

By the south porch of thatched Great Livermere church is the gravestone of William Saking, who died in 1689. He was a 'forkner' (falconer) to both King Charles II and to King James II.

The Walk

From the Bull take the road to Great Livermere and, in about ½ mile, immediately before the first house on the right, leave the road and walk on a headland path which leads to a children's playground. Continue now with the hedge on the right, and go into a lane, past some garages and swing left out to the road.

Turn right along the road and, when opposite a pair of flint cottages on your right, turn left on a grassy path which leads to the thatched church. Go left along a track and in a few yards turn right by a footpath sign, betwen a pair of lodges with brick gate pillars. Walk on this broad, stony track for ¼ mile. Immediately after crossing the bridge between two lakes go over a stile and keep on, still on the track. At the field boundary go through a gate or over the adjacent stile and continue on the track for just under ½ mile, until you are not quite level with the corner of a wood away on your left.

Turn left off the track, at right angles to it, and walk almost parallel with the edge of the wood on your right. Aim for the corner of the field at the edge of the wood. As you get nearer to the wood you will join a track. Keep on down until you reach the edge of a lake. Go right, through a substantial metal gate, then left on to the very long footbridge across Ampton Water.

At the far side go straight ahead into the woods, climbing slightly. Presently you come to a clearing ahead, with an enclosure for young game birds, made of high chicken wire. Follow the wire on your left for a long way as you go through Oldbroom Plantation. Occasionally, low down, you will see grilles set in the fence that the birds can get through yet the foxes cannot, and an electric wire, also low down, as a further deterrent to foxes.

When the fence goes sharply left you go straight ahead, on a grassy

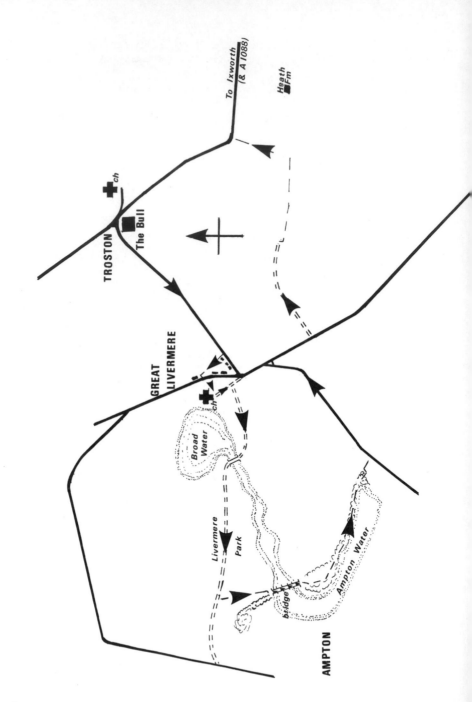

path through woodland, yet only a few yards from the field edge beyond a shallow ditch. In about 10 yards, by a waist-high metal rail, go left a yard or two and then continue as before. Do not go left across a footbridge.

Leave the woods, by a footpath sign. Go left for 30 yards on a grassy track and turn right over a culvert with a handrail, and along the field edge out to the road by some white posts. This is the point where a Roman road crossed this road, going roughly east-west. Turn left along the road for about ¼ mile until you are nearly at a road junction in Great Livermere.

As you approach the junction swing right along a short track, which in 50 yards brings you to the road. Turn right, away from the village. Pass, on the left of the road and behind some white railings, a small tree-girt pond, and in 50 yards, at the bridleway sign, take the grassy track to the left.

In about ½ mile the wide grass track ends, and you swing right across a ditch on the right and then go left to follow a narrow headland path with the same ditch now on the left. Pass a bank which comes in obliquely from the left, and which forms the field boundary of the enormous field you have been skirting. In a further 300 yards, and in sight of a black barn with a red roof, a field away, turn left over a sleeper cartbridge and follow a field boundary on the right which comprises, at first, a very shallow ditch and some isolated oaks.

Continue beside the ditch and later a hedge, out to the road. Turn left and follow the road for about ½ mile into Troston and to the Bull.

Rougham
The Bennet Arms

Although close to Bury St Edmunds, Rougham is a tranquil village with a life of its own. One of the most notable features is the abundance of trees in the area, not woodland so much as lots and lots of mature trees in the hedgerows and standing alone in mid-field.

The Bennet Arms is popular and friendly. As well as the bar area at the front there is a very restful sun lounge at the back of the inn looking out on to the garden, where you may eat. There is also a large garden for al fresco drinking and for children's play. No dogs, please.

The pub, which was originally a pair of cottages, is at least 200 years old. It is a Greene King house, serving Greene King Mild beer and Blackthorn Dry cider. It differs from the other pubs in this book in that there is no written set menu. On enquiring what was available, the reply we got was 'Well, what would you like?' With the ball in our court, we sat down to delicious, tender lamb chops, new potatoes, mint sauce and vegetables for one of us, and plaice and chips for the other. No food is served on Mondays.

Telephone: 0359 70356.

How to get there: Rougham village lies a few miles south of the A14 Bury to Ipswich road. From the A14, take the junction for Beyton. At Beyton keep the village green on the right and go west along the Bury road. In a mile turn left on to a minor road to High Rougham for another mile, ignoring turns to the left, till you reach the Bennet Arms, in the centre of the village. (Do not follow signs for Rougham Industrial Estate which is on the opposite side of the dual carriageway.)

Parking: There is good parking at the rear of the Bennet Arms.

Length of the walk: 4 miles. Map: OS Landranger 155 Bury St Edmunds and Sudbury area (GR 917618).

The first part of the walk takes a well-used field path direct to St Mary's parish church. Its location, ½ mile from the village, may be due to the influence of a former owner of Rougham Hall, because the church lies almost midway between the village and the Hall. The route continues across arable farmland and pasture to a lake at the foot of Eastlow Hill. The lake, a haunt for anglers, is at the head of a tributary to the river Lark. Not far from the lake is the site of a Roman building, whilst at the top of Eastlow Hill are some ancient burial mounds. The return to the village is along headland paths and country lanes.

The Walk

Leave the Bennet Arms and go into the village along the Bury St Edmunds road, and in 200 yards, at the T-junction, turn right. Just at the edge of the village, the road swings sharply left and in about a further 100 yards, leave the road on a well-used grass path on the right. This leads out to a road close to the church. Turn left and enter the churchyard. Cross the churchyard diagonally, passing the tower, and leave by an iron gate in the far corner into the school field.

Cross the playing field and go through a kissing-gate into a large field. Keep to the headland path with a hedge on the left until you are confronted by a substantial cross-hedge. Turn left in front of the hedge, cross a sleeper bridge and continue on a headland with the hedge on the right. Almost directly under the electricity grid wires, turn right over another bridge and, keeping on the headland, you soon reach the road.

Cross straight over and, keeping in the same direction, continue, first with a hedge on the left and then, at an oak tree, on the right. At the field boundary cross a bridge and then a stile into a meadow. Veer slightly left and make for a stile beside a gate, midway along the opposite hedge line. Go across a small field, following the hedge on the left, and out through another gate into a large pasture where,

29

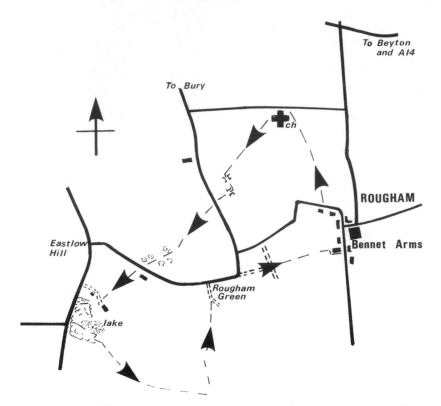

To Beyton
and A14

To Bury

ch

ROUGHAM

Eastlow
Hill

Bennet Arms

Rougham
Green

lake

keeping roughly in the same direction, and after passing several large old oak trees, go over a stile, out to a road near the thatched and pargeted Lake Farm House.

Turn right along the road for about 40 yards and then turn left off the road through a gate. Walk almost diagonally across the meadow and through a gap in the far hedge. It may mean climbing over a poorly fixed iron gate. Cross the arable field on a line parallel to the hedge on the left, making for the left-hand end of a row of young cupressus trees and about 25 yards to the right of the thatched cottage ahead. On the far side find a sleeper bridge across a ditch. This leads into the garden of Lake Cottage. In 10 yards come to the drive leading to the house. Here, bear almost half-right and, crossing the lawn, make for the far end of a well-trimmed hedge which borders the lawn on the right. When you reach the hedge, continue with it on your right and cross into another garden where you will see the lake a few yards away on the left. Cross another well-cut lawn to a stile about 20 yards away and enter some woods. Follow the path at the edge of the woods, with a fence on the right, to come out to Eastlow Hill Road.

Turn left on the road for about 100 yards until a road joins from the right. At this point turn left into a wooded area beside the lake. Skirt the edge of the lake, keeping it on your left. When you reach the corner, at a waymark, turn right, away from the water to the edge of the wood. Swing round to the left, keeping just inside the wood. It is a narrow, somewhat meandering path which shortly leads into a poplar plantation. Keep along by a row of poplars and, at the far left-hand corner of the plantation, take a narrow path through a blackthorn spinney, over a plank bridge and into an open field.

For the next ¼ mile follow a headland path (hedge on the left), crossing a sleeper bridge over a ditch on three occasions. Just before reaching a fourth cross-ditch, there are a few isolated trees along the ditch. Turn left and cross a sleeper bridge to go through the hedge which you have been following for the last ¼ mile. You are at the corner of a field. Now take a wide headland path, with a ditch and hedge on the right, which leads into a green lane. When you reach the tarmac drive keep straight on and in 150 yards, at the T-junction, turn right along the road.

Where the road bends sharply left, go straight ahead on a green lane. After passing some houses on the right, the lane becomes a grassy track with a hedge on the left. When you meet another track at right angles, go left for a few yards and then right on to a wide, well-used headland path. The path continues, first with a hedge on the left, then on the right, and, finally, as a cross-field path leading to a pedestrian gate.

Skirt a row of bungalows and out to a road, then turn left into the village and in 200 yards turn right, back to the start.

Other local attractions: To the north-west of the village, and very close to the A14, is Blackthorpe Barn. This ancient timber-built, thatched, semi-aisled barn is over 100 ft long and about 30 ft wide. The cavernous structure was built about 1550, and up until 1985 was in use as a grain store. It is now used for exhibitions, lectures, craft markets and Christmas tree sales in season. For details of what's on and when, ring 0359 70238.

7 Lavenham
The Angel

Lavenham is a town which most visitors to Suffolk want to see. It was made rich by the medieval wool trade and has streets which seem to have changed little over hundreds of years. Timber-framed buildings abound; few towns can have as many as Lavenham. In the Market Place is the Guildhall, an early 16th century Tudor, timber-framed building. Also in the Market Place is ochre-washed Little Hall, the headquarters of the Suffolk arm of the Council for the Preservation of Rural England. Both of these are open to the public, as is the Priory in Water Street.

The Angel has stood in one corner of the Market Place, overlooking the Guildhall and the Market Cross, since 1420. It is a large inn, but not impersonal. The bar is an island, with plenty of space and a dining area all round it. When the bar was refurbished, a double inglenook Tudor fireplace was discovered, and when restoration work took place in the 1950s a Tudor shuttered shop window was exposed. As could be expected of an inn first licensed 570 years ago, there are a lot of sturdy oak beams. A games area is at the rear of the bar.

The menu is changed daily and always includes locally smoked meat and fish, and at least one vegetarian dish. There are such delights as

Suffolk ham and cheese pie, Suffolk apple flan, pork and apples in cider, lamb chops marinated in garlic and rosemary, sirloin steak pan-fried in butter, mushroom tart, grilled fresh sardines, hazelnut meringue, and ice-cream with stem ginger. Real ales served are Nethergate Bitter, Courage Directors, Webster's and Ruddles County. Strongbow draught cider is available. A large beer garden can be found behind the inn, reached through the coaching entrance. There is a family room for children and dogs are welcome.

Telephone: 0787 247388.

How to get there: Lavenham is about 10 miles south of Bury St Edmunds, on the A1141 road. The Angel is in the Market Place, which is a short distance from the main road through the village and reached by turning north off Water Street along Lady Street.

Parking: There is parking in the Market Place and also two big public car parks, one of which is close behind the Angel and reached from Prentice Street, beside the inn.

Length of the walk: 3 miles. Map: OS Landranger 155 Bury St Edmunds and Sudbury (GR 916493).

The walk goes in a semicircle to the north of the town. It includes part of the Lavenham Railway Walk, managed for the public to enjoy by Suffolk County Council, along the line of the former Lavenham to Sudbury railway, which closed in 1967. Pleasant field paths make up much of the rest of the route.

The Walk

From the Angel, walk across the Market Place and descend the narrow Market Lane to the High Street. Turn right and walk down the hill. In about 300 yards note on your left a delightful modern, carved corner-post, and a frieze above it, depicting many wild creatures. A note in the window below says, 'With the exception of the lynx all these creatures still roam freely in Great Britain.' On the opposite side of the road see a pair of March hares silhouetted, boxing, on a metal street sign. Looking up left into Roper's Court you will see the old maltings on the right, with its white-boarded lucam.

Keep on the main road on a broad footway, with a grassy bank sloping to the road on your right. At the bottom of the hill, before the road climbs again to go over the former railway bridge, and just after No 53, Driftside, on the left, go left a little and take the footpath between a hedge on the left and the bank beside the road on the right.

The level path swings round to the left to reach the former railway line. Follow the old railway for just over ¼ mile and by a metal wicket

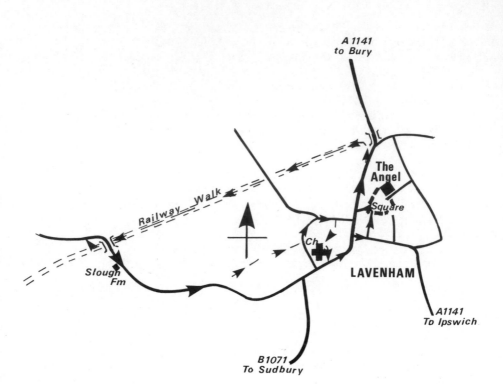

gate reach a road, Park Road. Cross it and go through another wicket gate to rejoin the railway track. Later pass under a three-arch bridge which takes a road over the path, and immediately go up a steepish ramp on the right, with a handrail.

The ramp leads directly up to a layby. Looking north, see a whitewashed cottage with two gables, and notice in each gable the two pentice boards which are designed to throw rainwater pouring down the gable, out and away from the walls. These are fairly common on old cottages.

Turn right and go over the bridge, the one you have just walked under, and carry on along the road, Bridge Street Road. This is not the tautology it seems, as it is in fact the road to the place called Bridge Street.

As the road begins a slow bend to the right, take the public footpath which goes off at an angle on the left, heading to the left of the distant church in Lavenham. Follow the broad, grassy path till you join a road by a stile next to a wooden farm gate. The church is on your right, but

34

you go left along the road. Pass a farmhouse on the left, dated 1897. Keep right at a junction, Park Road, and then, by a triple-gabled brick house, dated 1873, turn right off the road through a gap in a brick wall.

Go down a path between a wall and an iron fence, over a little bridge and through a gate with an iron scroll above it. Follow the iron fence on the right as it curves round towards the church. There is an enormous horse chestnut tree here. Enter the churchyard through a carved wooden kissing-gate, and notice the strong smell of box, from the many box bushes, redolent of an old-fashioned English country garden.

Walk out of the churchyard into Church Street and go left. Pass Tenter Piece on your left. This land was where wooden frames called 'tenters' were set up. After being washed, the woollen cloth was stretched out on the tenters, held firmly by tenter hooks, and left to dry. (Hence the phrase 'being on tenterhooks'.)

Walk into the village. At the Elizabethan Swan Hotel turn right into Water Street and then go left, opposite the Priory, into Lady Street, to return to the Market Place.

Other local attractions: Dominating the Market Square is the Guildhall, owned by the National Trust. In it is an exhibition of local history and local industry, including a comprehensive display about the cloth industry. It is open from the end of March until the beginning of November. Ring 0787 247646 for times. There are also several art galleries in Lavenham.

Walsham le Willows
8 The Blue Boar Inn

Walsham le Willows is a compact, interesting village. Whilst the houses fronting the main street are of a wide variety of styles and sizes, taken together these buildings make up a delightfully integrated scene. The various colour-washed houses blend one with another. Some are blue, some white, pink, yellow-ochre, and some green-washed. A broad stream flows westward through the village, flanking the main street at its eastern end. Nearby and almost opposite the school, the former maltings have been imaginatively converted into an award-winning range of dwellings which are worth seeing.

The blue boar was the sign of the Earls of Oxford. The white boar was the sign of the House of York. It is said that when Richard III was defeated by Henry VII at the Battle of Bosworth many white boar signs were hastily repainted blue, as the Earl of Oxford, whose badge that was, supported Henry Tudor. This Blue Boar Inn has a very pleasant main bar area with old beams and a large inglenook fireplace, where a log fire crackles with a warm welcome on dull winter days. There is an adjacent restaurant, which has walls covered in horseracing pictures and mementos, including racing silks. The landlord is very knowledgeable about the turf. The inn was the 'local' for the

13th Squadron at Honington, as the pictures in the bar show. Most of the food is home-cooked. Fish is a favourite dish here, coming straight from Lowestoft. Dover sole, lemon sole, wing of skate, salmon trout, halibut steaks, swordfish steaks and goujons of plaice are usually on the menu. There are also steak, ale and mushroom pie, turkey, ham and mushroom pie, grilled gammon, chicken cordon bleu, and strawberry meringue, treacle tart and apple pie – just to whet your appetite. Meals are not available on Sunday evenings.

Real ales such as Theakston Best, Greene King IPA, Adnams and Tolly Original, and Strongbow cider are served here. Outside are a terrace and a large garden, with plenty of children's play equipment. Dogs, however, are best left in the car.

Telephone: 0359 258889.

How to get there: Walsham le Willows is 5 miles east of Ixworth and is signposted from the A143. The Blue Boar is in the main street, close to the church.

Parking: There is parking at the front of the Blue Boar, and also a village car park (Trust the Motorist charge) 100 yards further down the main street on the south side.

Length of the walk: 3 miles. Map: OS Landranger 155 Bury St Edmunds and Sudbury (GR 001712).

This is an easy walk, through the attractive village and on by good field paths, green lanes, mixed woodland and meadows in a gently undulating landscape, well provided with mature hedges and with a chocolate-box view of a cottage across the fields now and again.

In the main street see how many houses take their names from trees.

The Walk

From the Blue Boar turn right and walk along the main street until the road snakes left by the Congregational chapel. Keep on the right side of the road here, go over the little bridge and continue on a footway, with the stream on your left. At the next bridge on the left, by Clarkes, go left and meet the road again.

Cross straight over and, with a white cottage end-on to the road at the corner, go along a track with cupressus trees on the left and a 7 ft high flint wall on the right. Pass a few cottages and snake left and right on the farm track, with a hedge on the right and a ditch on the left. Later, ignore a wide culvert on the right that takes a path over to a cluster of houses away to the right. Pass under some electricity wires, and on until, just after a pond on the right, you meet a farm

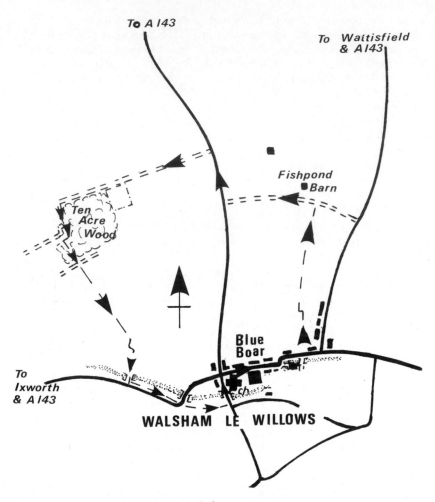

track at a T-junction. Turn left.

Follow this track, with old Fishpond Barn and later Fishpond Farm away to your right, and soon meet a road. Go right, pass a cream-washed house on the left and, opposite the track leading to Fishpond Farm, go left through the pedestrian gate beside the stile in the post-and-rail fence. Carry on along this headland track, with mature trees on the left, past relics of wartime England, and alongside a wood to its end.

Go left beside the wood, on round a dog-leg to the right and continue until you are within 50 yards of the cross-hedge ahead. Here go left over a culvert into the woods and in 10 yards turn right, over a two-plank footbridge and then later cross a culvert and turn right, beside a fence on the left and a ditch on your right, for about 50 yards. Turn left and walk with a single strand of wire on your left, about 3 yards within the wood, until you reach an old concrete farm track. Cross straight over.

Continue, with a mature hedge on the left, along this wavy field margin. At the hedge end there is a small clearing with a lump of concrete in the centre. Go more or less straight on, snaking left a little over the lump of concrete into a small grove of trees, with a grassy path through it.

Soon ahead is a pond. Skirt to the right of it and then bear right with a post-and-rail fence on your right and a hedge on the left. Go over a stile, cross a farm track and go over another stile onto a wooden footbridge. Immediately go left over yet another stile – not over the stile ahead that would take you on to the road.

Walk through a wide belt of light woodland, with the stream down on your left and the road hidden away on the right. At the end go out to a stile which is well recessed. Cross over the road to a short length of the old road. Take care, as it bends here, and the sight-lines are not good. In the section of old road go over a small wooden footbridge and through a kissing-gate into a meadow. Follow the post-and-rail fence on the left, with the stream below, and when in a tongue of land go rightish towards a holly hedge to leave the meadow by a stile in the corner.

On the road, The Causeway, go left, over a brick bridge and past the Priory Room, up to the church. A path across the churchyard leads to the Blue Boar again.

Other local attractions: Around August Bank Holiday time Walsham le Willows has a Gardens Festival, when as many as 28 of the pretty gardens in the village are open to the public.

9 Chelsworth
The Peacock Inn

Chelsworth lies in the broad valley of the river Brett. As the village is not on a main route to anywhere, unless you count the Bildeston to Monks Eleigh road, it is quiet and unspoilt. Lots of colour-washed, thatched cottages add charm to the village street.

The Peacock Inn can trace its history back to 1390. It is a welcoming pub, with a log fire burning in its vast fireplace in winter, the sweet, pungent smell of wood smoke scenting the air even under the trees by the river meadow opposite. For warm, sunny days there is a beer garden, with a garden bar for children, serving soft drinks and ice-cream. Accommodation is available. Specialities of the house are home-made pies and traditional Sunday roasts. Some of the other items on the menu are apple and Stilton soup, steak and ale pie, vegetable quiche, lamb steak, sirloin steak, chilli con carne, lasagne with salad and french fries and chicken with barbecue sauce. This freehouse, which is open all day, can offer six real ales, Courage Directors, Marston's Pedigree, Wadworths 6X, Courage Best, John Smith's and Adnams. If you want draught cider you can choose between Scrumpy Jack and Dry Blackthorn.

Well-behaved dogs on leads are welcome.

Telephone: 0449 740758.

How to get there: Chelsworth is about 15 miles south-east of Bury St Edmunds, and can be reached from the A1141 road between Hadleigh and Lavenham. At the point, on the eastern edge of Monks Eleigh, where the the A1141 makes a right angle turn, turn off towards Bildeston on the B1115. Chelsworth is just 1 mile away, with the Peacock in the main street.

Parking: There is a car park behind the pub, also a limited amount of parking by the telephone box just opposite the inn.

Length of the walk: 2½ miles. Map: OS Landranger 155 Bury St Edmunds and Sudbury (GR 981480).

This leisurely short walk starts along the Chelsworth village street, which is fronted by many old thatched cottages, colour-washed in a variety of pastel shades. A short diversion to All Saints church, passing the Tudor Chelsworth Grange, is recommended.
The route follows a stream for a short distance, then crosses the river Brett. Thereafter it goes through the park of Chelsworth Hall, climbing the slight hill to the south of the village where good views of the surrounding area can be seen. To return to the village the walk descends to the river Brett near Nedging Mill, and follows the watermeadows to picturesque Chelsworth bridge.

The Walk
From the Peacock go along the road, in the direction of Monks Eleigh. The orangey-brown-washed building by the church is the Grange. This is a collection of many buildings with as many styles. In an open-air museum in Holland there is a house described as a Good Year House – whenever the owner had a good year he extended his house, adding a bit here and a bit there. The development of the Grange is somewhat like that. All the parts blend harmoniously together. On the right at the next bend is The Old Schoolhouse, with a large window in the east end. Away up the hill on the left is Chelsworth Hall which you will pass closer to later. Near the end of the village, the road crosses a stream, a tributary of the river Brett, sometimes called the Wagger. Nearby on the right, beside Cakebridge Lane, is an old weaver's cottage, characterised by the two wide windows, barely 2 ft high, which would have given extra light to the loom. Opposite the cottage there is an old carved post at the corner of a building.

Just after Cakebridge Lane, but before crossing the road bridge over the stream, leave the road and go left down the footpath to walk beside the river on your right. Notice the attractively designed modern house on the left, fitting tastefully into the village scene. Curve round with the stream, cross a brick footbridge and go over a stile into

41

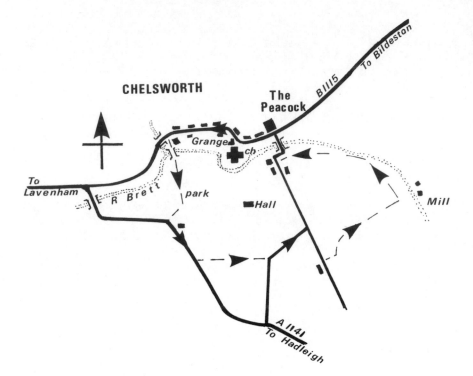

Chelsworth Park. Under the large old ash tree, stand and look across the park to a brick house with two cream gables on the far side. Head towards the right of that house.

After crossing a shallow stream you will be able to see the stile in the far fence, a little to the left of the transformer on a pole. Go over the stile, up to the layby, and on up the hill on the road. Take care as it is sometimes busy and there are no verges. When it levels out and the wood on the left ends, go left off the road by a wide gap into the corner of a field. Follow the headland path, with a shelter belt on the left.

Meet a road at a bend. Away to your left is Chelsworth Hall. Walk on down the road to a T-junction. Ahead on the horizon is the white water tower on Wattisham airfield. Turn right and walk along the road as far as the first building on your right. You are now up by Chelsworth Common. Leave the road here, going down a green sunken lane on your left.

Follow the curving lane as it drops. You enter the bottom left corner of a poplar plantation and go on along the track, down into light woodland with a deep pit on the right at the bottom, planted with many young trees. Climb up into the corner of an open field with Nedging Mill straight ahead. Walk down beside the sparse hedge to the black two-step stile. Go over it into a small field, which you cross to another stile and so into a very big field.

Walk ahead for 100 yards or so, over towards the woodland by Nedging Mill. Turn left in the field and walk roughly parallel to the left boundary for a long way, curving slowly left. Eventually the field narrows and you have the river beside you on the right as you go over a wooden stile beside a wooden gate. Continue parallel to the left hedge to the end of the field. Go over the wooden stile and walk out between fences to the road.

Turn right and snake round along the road, over the two bridges over the Brett, and so back to the Peacock.

Other local attractions: In late June almost the whole village collaborates in an Open Garden scheme, when for the price of one ticket which covers parking, one may wander through the village, in and out of all the participating gardens. Afternoon teas are available and plants are for sale.

10 Stoke-by-Nayland
The Black Horse

At the top of a hill overlooking the Stour valley to the south and the valley of the river Box, a tributary of the Stour, to the north, stands the village of Stoke-by-Nayland. This compact village with its many groups of attractive cottages is dominated at its centre by St Mary's church whose 120 ft high tower is a landmark for many miles around. The settlement is formed by a square of four short roads from which country lanes radiate to the neighbouring villages and hamlets. It is a rural area with gentle hills and green river valleys.

The attractive Black Horse buildings, which are in the village centre, are around 400 years old, and have been a public house for the last 100 years. The inn specialises in Indian food. Such dishes as murgh ka salan – a hot chicken curry – Penang beef curry, aloo gosht – a lamb curry – and chicken makhan are on the menu. To follow, there is a wide range of puddings. In addition, a curry night is held once a month, for which booking is essential. The set meal, an authentic Asian menu, is different each time and recipes are drawn from various regions, including Thailand and Malaysia. Food is not served on Mondays. At this freehouse real ales, such as Greene King IPA, Rayments and Abbot, are available. There is no family room, neither is there a garden area, but children dining with their parents are welcome. Dogs may be taken into the public bar. Quoits are played in the field adjoining the pub.

Telephone: 0206 262504.

How to get there: Stoke-by-Nayland is on the minor B1068 road, which runs from the A12 trunk road near Stratford St Mary to Leavenheath, a village 6 miles from Sudbury on the A134 Sudbury to Colchester road.

Parking: There is parking behind the pub.

Length of the walk: 3½ miles. Map: OS Landranger 155 Bury St Edmunds and Sudbury (GR 988363).

From the hilltop of Stoke-by-Nayland the walk descends over headland paths to the river Box. Having crossed the river, it continues across parkland and through woods to the ridge on the north side of the Box valley. From here, the way drops down to the tree-fringed village pond of Polstead. The return is by way of Polstead church, Polstead bridge and across farmland, climbing the hill again.

The Walk

From the crossroads near the Black Horse, take the road towards Higham and Ipswich. In about 300 yards and at the first field boundary, turn left and follow the high hedge on the left. At the bottom of the hill keep beside the hedge as it swings round to the right. (Do not follow the well-walked path which goes left through the hedge.)

Eventually your headland path ends at a short length of rough ground with a small poplar grove on the right. Go straight on into a large field and head across it in nearly the same direction towards the mid point of the hedge in the valley. When you reach that hedge make a U-turn to the left and walk along the headland with the hedge on your right.

Go through a gap in a cross-hedge and keep in the same direction, now with a shallow ditch on the right, towards a group of farm buildings. About 30 yards from the black converted barn, swing half-right through 10 yards of rough ground, over a stile and cross a small meadow to a stile which leads out to a road.

Turn right along the road, pass the large and attractive building, Scotland Place, cross the river and very soon, opposite another fine building, Scotland House, turn left at a footpath sign and go over a bridge and a stile into a pasture. Continue roughly parallel to a line of willows on the left and you will reach the end of a row of mature trees,

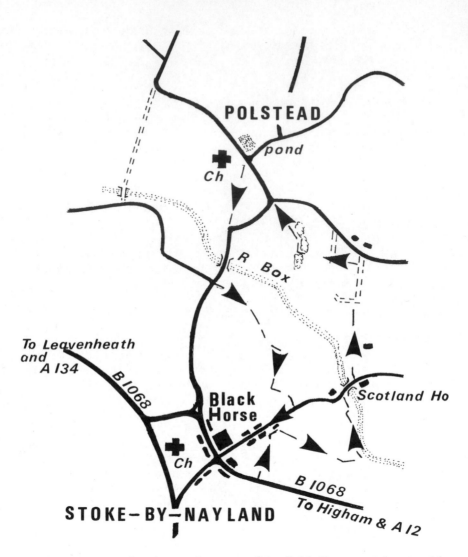

near to a gate and an internal corner of the field. Keep straight on with the trees and the field boundary on the right until you reach a stile, followed by a sleeper bridge.

· The path leads on through some rough land into another meadow. Here follow the field boundary, part hedge, part wooden fence, on the right. Cross the fence by a stile then cross a sleeper bridge and turn left to follow the ditch on the left. Very soon swing left to cross a wide culvert over the same ditch and climb rough ground to enter the

46

woods at a stile. Follow a narrow path as it winds through the woods. Halfway along, the path makes a sharp right turn at a waymark and leads out to meet a cart track at right angles. Turn right and very soon the track bends to the left up a hill.

At the top of the hill, and when you are a short distance from a house you can see ahead, turn left and keep along the top of the hill, with the ground on your left sloping down increasingly more steeply, to cross a stile which is visible at the far corner of the field. Turn right along a tarmac drive for about 10 yards and then turn left into a field, walking with a fence on the right to cross another stile in the shadow of some large trees.

You are now in the corner of a large, grassy pasture on the side of a hill where there are wide views of the village of Polstead. Turn right and follow the hedge on the right along the contour. Continue to follow the hedge as it bends to the left but, when it makes a sharp turn to the right, go straight on down the hill towards Polstead, passing close to an electricity pole in the middle of the field and continuing in the same direction, to reach the road at Bells Corner.

Walk straight on up the road for about 300 yards. When you come to the road junction, your way is to the left through a kissing-gate. But, before continuing your walk, spend a little time enjoying the peaceful Polstead pond which is just to the north of this junction. The kissing-gate leads into a field known as the Horse Croft. See the church away to your right and, passing two large oak trees, walk towards a white cottage on the far side of the field. Go to the right-hand side of the cottage and join a road at a bend.

Follow the road ahead and shortly cross the river Box at Polstead bridge. A little further on, and almost opposite Mill Lane on the right, turn left at the footpath sign and go along a meadow with a hedge on the right. Continue to the left of the hedge for several fields. At the end of the first field there is a wide gap leading into the second field. A narrow gap in a cross-hedge leads into the third field, at the far end of which is a row of willow trees.

At a waymark about 50 yards before the willows, turn right through a gap in the hedge and go up the hill along a crop division. At the top of the field swing round to the left and continue to the next corner of the field where, at a waymark, you turn right and enter a wood. The path bends to the left and over two sleeper bridges. Keep going in the same general direction and, after crossing a stile, you reach the road. Turn right and walk back ½ mile into Stoke-by-Nayland and your starting point.

⓫ Onehouse
The Shepherd and Dog

The Rattlesden river flows for 8 miles eastward from Felsham into the Gipping at Stowmarket. The Shepherd and Dog stands close to the river, just by Burford bridge, almost midway between the villages of Onehouse and Great Finborough. The river valley is surrounded by arable farmland, but alongside the Rattlesden there are woods and meadows, and on the slope of the hill rising to Great Finborough church is the Stowmarket golf course.

This popular pub has existed since about 1500. It had its own brewery at the rear of the pub, which was working until the pub was sold to Greene King in 1879. It has a pleasant outlook and a quiet and intimate dining area. The real ales are IPA and Abbot. Taunton Dry Blackthorn cider is also available. Lunches are served every day of the week from 12 noon till 2 pm but there are no evening meals. The menu is wide and changes frequently. Such fare as lasagne, plaice dippers, chicken or bacon pancakes, haddock or cod fillets and chicken nuggets is on offer, together with a variety of puddings. There is a children's menu, and vegetarian dishes are available. Behind the pub is an excellent play area for children. Dogs are not permitted inside the pub.

Telephone: 0449 612698.

How to get there: The Shepherd and Dog at Onehouse is just over a mile west of Stowmarket, and about 50 yards from the bridge over the Rattlesden on the B1115 Great Finborough road.

Parking: There is parking to the front and the side of the Shepherd and Dog.

Length of the walk: 4 miles. Map: OS Landranger 155 Bury St Edmunds and Sudbury (GR 026587).

The walk circles a part of the Rattlesden river valley between Onehouse and Great Finborough, over pleasant, undulating country, farmland, woods and part of the Stowmarket golf course. The going is easy. The spire of St Andrew's church can be seen as a landmark for most of the circuit.

The golf course is a wide open area, interspersed with clumps of shrubs and mature trees. The route of the public path, though not immediately apparent on the ground, lies across the golf course. In walking, avoid the greens and before crossing the fairways, look left and right for golfers about to drive the ball.

The Walk
From the Shepherd and Dog, turn left on the road to the T-junction, then right and over Burford bridge. When just past the next T-junction on the left, Combs Lane, leave the road, going right, into a field. Turn right and follow the fence to the Rattlesden river and then turn left and keep close to the river bank, along the edge of several fields, for about ½ mile. Turn away from the stream with the thick hedge on the right. In about 200 yards turn right, over a stile on to the golf course.

Walk parallel to the golf course boundary, round to the right until you reach the fourth tee, half-tucked into woodland, then turn left across the golf course, past five young copper beeches, to some low spreading cotoneaster shrubs which lie close to the edge of the fairway. Just before the bushes, turn half-left and head up the hill towards the tall, slender, banded spire of Great Finborough church, which you can just see amongst the trees.

When you reach a tarmac track, go left towards the school buildings, but keep within the golf course by veering to the right along the boundary. Pass all the buildings on your left and, immediately after the last low school building, swing left and enter the school grounds by a farm gate. Carry on within the grounds alongside an iron fence until quite near the church. By a metal kissing-gate on the right leave the grounds and go out into the field, following the field edge path round past the west end of the church. Swing left, over a stile into a lane alongside the south side of the church, to join a tarmac road.

Bear right and walk out to Great Finborough village. Pass the

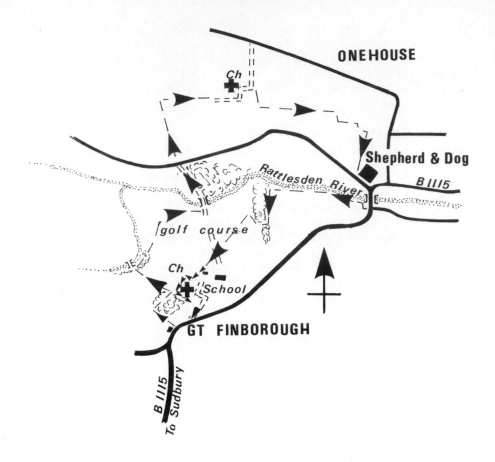

Chestnut Horse pub and continue along the road, almost as far as the post office. Immediately before it, go right over a wooden stile, beside a metal gate. Walk across the field to the far corner by the left end of a small wood, and leave the field by a kissing-gate. Go right for 2 yards, then right again into the woods and go left along a path inside the woods, which takes you to a field near the west end of the church.

Where four paths meet, go left with the hedge on the left, down the hill. Where the hedge turns left, look across the field and see in the valley bottom a long thin line of woodland. Head for a point near the middle of the woodland. You may be able to see a farmhouse on the horizon above the trees. Aim for that.

When you get near the valley bottom you will see a dog-leg in the edge of the woodland. Make for the inner corner of the dog-leg and turn right down the bank, then go over a small stream. In a yard or so you will see on your left a footbridge – do not go that way, but go right a little and then ahead on a path that meanders through light woodland, with the river on your left, to emerge in 50 yards in a corner of the golf course.

Keep to the right of the green, with the hedge on the right. Keep straight on, and continue with the shallow ditch and a few trees on your right. Presently the ditch curves round to the right, with a hill on the right. Pass beside clumps of mature chestnut trees, and on along a track now, passing the third tee, until you meet a tarmac track at right angles. Here, go left and cross a bridge of white bricks, over the river Rattlesden.

Where the track divides, keep left and follow the path all the way up the hill, and out, between big brick pillars and iron gates, to join the road.

Go left a few yards on the road, then, opposite Cedar House, leave the road again, going right, with the hedge on the right, up the hill. Walk up to a plateau, passing under two sets of electricity wires. Away to your right is E-shaped, gabled Onehouse Hall.

By a cross-ditch on the right, turn right over a culvert and walk with the ditch on your right along the grassy farm track. At the field end go through a very wide gap in the cross-hedge ahead, turn right for 20 yards, then left, climbing slightly, with a hedge on your right. Ahead is the church of St John the Baptist, Onehouse.

Follow the broad track round past the church, with post-and-rail fences on your right, and when by the east end of the church, keep right on the track, with the hedge on the right. At the end of that field, where the track turns left, pass a pair of very wide metal gates on the right and go straight on through a gap. Turn right and walk south, with the hedge on the right. At the field end, beside barns on the right, go through a gap in the cross-hedge ahead and turn left.

Follow the grassy farm track with the hedge on the left. When the hedge turns left, snake left very slightly and continue in the same direction as before on a path between fields towards houses in the distance. At the field end go right with the hedge on the left, to a point where that hedge goes left and you go left with it.

Presently, the path wiggles right, round a bulge and then meets a cross-hedge. Do not go through, but turn right and walk along the field edge, with the hedge on the left, to the corner and beyond out to the road beside the Shepherd and Dog.

12 Redgrave
The Cross Keys

Two rivers form the northern boundary of Suffolk. The Waveney flows eastward towards Lowestoft and the North Sea, whilst the Little Ouse flows westwards to the Great Ouse and thence out to The Wash. The sources of both these rivers lie within yards of each other in a marshy swamp, now a nature reserve, known as Redgrave and Lopham Fens. Redgrave, just south of the fen, is a pretty village with many old thatched, whitewashed cottages. Most of the present thatch is straw, but when the cottages were first built, the reeds from the nearby fen were probably used for the village roofs.

The Cross Keys, a freehouse with good food and a warm friendly welcome, runs a popular quiz on Sunday evenings; not the intense league type of competition, but a fun quiz. Weekly in summer there is an unusual barbecue where the pub supplies the food and the customers cook it themselves. It is a well-attended event. Morris dancers visit the pub about four times a year, including Boxing Day. This is a colourful, jolly occasion alongside the village green. On the menu of this 500-year-old pub are such dishes as butterfly prawns as a starter, with a good selection of main courses including gammon, egg and chips, sirloin and T-bone steaks, whilst you may finish with such delicacies as nut cream pie, hot chocolate fudge cake, treacle sponge, lemon brûlée, and fruit pies. A selection of children's meals is also served. Meals are not available on Mondays, or on Sunday evenings. The real ales are Adnams, Greene King IPA and Abbot, as well as guests. Draught cider is on offer too.

Dogs are allowed in the garden only.

Telephone: 0379 898510.

How to get there: Redgrave is 5 miles west of Diss and is on the B1113, which runs between Botesdale on the A143 and South Lopham on the A1066. The Cross Keys is in the centre of the village by the green.

Parking: There is a car park at the rear of the Cross Keys. It is also possible to park beside the green.

Length of the walk: 3½ miles. Map: OS Landranger 144 Thetford and Breckland (GR 045780).

This is an easy stroll, mostly on good, well-used tracks. From the green, by the Cross Keys, take a lane nearby which leads northward to the Redgrave Fen Nature Reserve. Here the route follows a short length of the Angles Way, a long-distance path along the Waveney valley, on a permissive path within the reserve. Go through woods of oak and birch skirting the wide reed beds, the haunt of marsh-loving creatures and plants, and allow some time to explore the path further. Leaving the fen, the path follows a track, known expressively as Bier Lane, to Redgrave church and thence in a wide sweep, back to the village.

The Walk

Leave the pub, going left on the road to Diss, alongside the village green, and at the corner of the green keep left. In about 100 yards, by a transformer on a pole, go left off the road along a gravelled cart track. Pass a couple of bungalows on the left and keep on a well-used track with a hedge on the left. After passing a grassy footpath going off right, the track continues, now a grassy headland path, to the corner of the field. The path swings slightly left then right, round the edge of a small wood. As you go downhill you can see the valley ahead. Pass a pinkish cottage on the right and join a gravel track between hedges out to the road. Cross straight over and join the Angles Way, along a wide track with hedges on both sides. Pass a barrier, and an informative board, into the Redgrave and Lopham Fens area – 300 acres of dense reed and sedge, waterways, woodland and paths.

The walk on the Angles Way through the nature reserve is by permission of the owners. Should the path be closed at any time, take

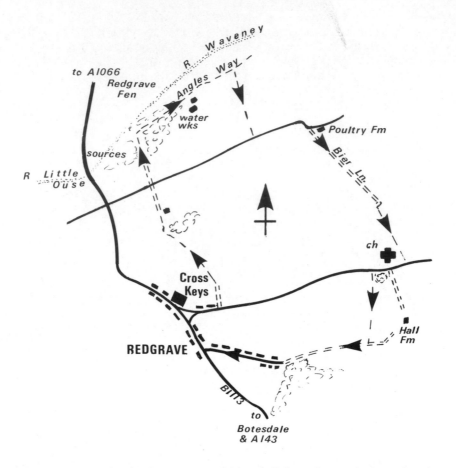

the minor road which runs roughly parallel to the path (see sketch map).

Follow the main path as it curves right through light woodland, with the reed beds away to the left. Pass on your right the low Suffolk Water Company building. Presently fork right a little, getting nearer to the edge of the wood among bracken now and very near a field boundary fence on the right. Near the corner of the field on the right, by another smaller notice board, turn right to leave the Angles Way.

If you have time, explore further into the nature reserve by going ahead on the Angles Way and then return to this spot.

Take the narrow grass path between a hedge and trees on the left and sheep netting on the right. Go on past a barn and out to the road. Turn left and pass whitewashed, pantile-roofed Fen Street Farm on the right. The road swings right and then left. At the bend, leave the road, going up a cart track between hedges and passing Poultry Farmhouse a little to the left. Keep on the track, along a green lane known as Bier Lane. After passing two ponds, one to the left and one to the right, the hedge on the left ends and the cart track continues along the broad headland of a large field.

At the end of the field the track goes through a hedge into another large field. Ahead there is a good view of Redgrave church. At this point the track becomes a grassy footpath. A few yards into the field, the path turns sharp right and, soon after, turns sharp left across the open field. After passing several mature trees on the right, you reach a road not far from the church.

Turn right along the road to pass the church, which is about a mile from the village centre. Perhaps its location has more to do with the convenience of the former squire, who lived at the Elizabethan mansion, Redgrave Hall, now demolished, than the population of the village itself. The tower of the church was built of red brick, but faced with white bricks from Woolpit in the late 1700s. Inside, it is surprisingly large and light. Just after the end of the churchyard wall just beyond the wood on the left, turn left, cross the sleeper footbridge and follow the hedge away from the road. On the left is the large, square, Victorian Hall Farm. At the end of the field come out on to a cart track from the farm and turn right, towards Redgrave.

On the left are mature trees, which later give way to woods. Further along there is an old ice-house, later made redundant by refrigerators. The cart track comes out to the end of a road by a thatched white farmhouse. Carry on along the road, passing many other picturesque thatched houses. Towards the end see Priory Cottage which was built in 1550. At the main road bear right, signed 'Thetford B1113', and walk back past the village green, with its high-pitched, roofed shelter to return to the Cross Keys.

13 Finningham
The White Horse

Finningham is a close-knit village in the middle of the county. Four roads form a large square of houses. The White Horse is at one of the corners, and in the middle of the square is the church and an attractive recreation area, for both young and old.

The White Horse is orientated as much towards meals as to ale and cider. It has a friendly, cosy image and very soft, unobtrusive music plays. There are several small dining areas, carpeted and with dark beams. Even the loos are well appointed. The blackboard-menu is a work of art, printed by the landlord. The food, mainly home-made, is delicious and plentiful. Home-made soup, chicken liver pâté, garlic mushrooms, fillet, rump and sirloin steak, vegetarian dishes, home-made lasagne, chicken curry kashmiri with poppadums, syrup sponge pudding, spotted dick and custard, cheesecake and much more besides. Real ales are served, for example Tolly Original, Tetley Biter and Flowers IPA. Draught cider, Dry Blackthorn, is on offer too. There is a garden area for the children and dogs are welcome in the garden only.

Telephone: 0449 781250.

How to get there. Finningham lies on the B1113, about 3 miles west of the Stoke Ash crossroads on the A140.

Parking: The White Horse has a large car park.

Length of the walk: 3½ miles. Map: OS Landranger 155 Bury St Edmunds and Sudbury (GR 065692).

The walk circles the village. To the south of the village, just after going over the railway, there once stood a windmill. The site for a windmill often suggests a high point and good views. This is true here.

The Walk

Take the B1113 road northwards towards Walsham, and in 50 yards bear right along a footpath towards the church. Cross the recreation ground diagonally and get to the church. Leave the churchyard at the northern end and take the bridleway which is almost opposite. Go over the concrete bridlebridge, emerge on a road and turn right.

Pass Church Mouse Barn and go to the end of this short road. Go right a little, then left along a surfaced lane, with a stream on the right. Walk up to the iron gates, flanked by brick walls, of Frazer House and there go left on a farm track, a sunken green lane, with the stream on the right. Go under the brick railway arch and carry on, still with the stream on the right.

Walk out from this byway to join a very minor road, go to the right and in 200 yards meet a bigger road. Cross over and go straight ahead between fences. In a bit, go through another gate into a big odd-shaped field. Walk ahead and a little to the right, keeping the fenced stream on your left. Pass through a cross-hedge by a wide gap. See how the old trees beside the stream have been cut down and younger ones planted.

At the next cross-hedge go ahead, with the stream still on the left, into a scrubby area. Leave that field at the far end by a gap into the rounded corner of a very big field, with a water tower away in the distance half-right. Follow the field edge, with a deep ditch on the left. Go through a cross-hedge and walk to within 100 yards of the road ahead.

Here, where the track that you have been on goes on along a narrow band of land between a stream on the left and a hedge on the right, you turn right on a track with a hedge and ditch on the left. At the field end the track snakes right then left, and you now have a garden on your right. With hedges on both sides, you then pass thatched, pale pink Mill Cottage.

When the track comes to a T-junction, go right, still on a farm track

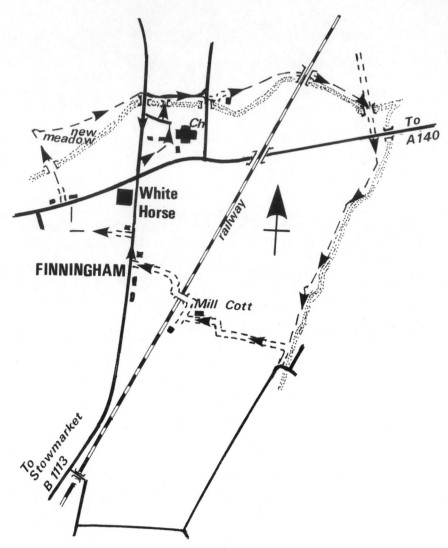

with hedges on both sides, and then left over the railway bridge. The track then swings right.

You are high up here and you have good views over Finningham and the surrounding country. This is where the tower mill used to be, before it was demolished in 1877. It was shown on a map of 1783, though it may have been there even earlier of course.

The track now curves round to the left and out to the road. Turn right, and, with care, walk along the road for 200 yards. By a small antique shop, turn left into a lane, a byway, with hedges on both sides. Keep straight on and, when within 40 yards of a clump of blackberries and a fence-line ahead and to the right, turn right, and stop a minute.

Look across the field to a bungalow with a low gable in the centre, not as high as the roof line, and a chimney towards the left end. Head across the field just to the right of this bungalow, and jump down the small bank to the road. Turn left for 15 yards and then turn right along a farm track, with the aforementioned bungalow on your right and a blue bungalow on your left. There is a hedge on the left for some while, and some old sheds. Keep on, cross a cart bridge and you will come to the corner of a very big field ahead.

Go straight on with a hedge and ditch on your right. At the far end of the field, walk out to another big field which extends both to the left and to the right. Turn right for a yard or so to the field corner. While you now go east you can use a permissive path along some of the Countryside Commission's 'Countryside Premium Scheme' land. Should this privilege be withdrawn for any reason, note that the public footpath still exists just on the other side, north, of the ditch.

With ditch, hedge and bank on the left, head towards the church tower, with the water tower half-right. At the skew cross-hedge, go through a gap about 5 yards from the corner, and continue as before with a shallow ditch on your left. At the corner of the field go past the metal gate into a green lane, with a bank on the left and a hedge on the right, and walk out to meet a road at a T-junction. Ahead you can see Church Mouse Barn again.

Turn right along the road, across the bridge over the stream, past the road to the church on the left, and back to the White Horse inn.

14 Barham
The Sorrel Horse

Barham is a small village on the side of the shallow Gipping valley. The river Gipping runs from north of Stowmarket down to Ipswich, where it flows into the head of the Orwell estuary, and reaches the sea between Felixstowe and Shotley. Shrubland Park extends for 4 miles along the eastern slope of the valley. It is part wood and part farmland. The Sorrel Horse is fairly large but divided by several features which give an intimate atmosphere to the interlinked areas. A huge log fire burns in the central fireplace from mildly cool autumn days onwards to spring. The pub food is excellent and reasonably priced. As well as a standard menu there is a different home-made dish every day, for instance lasagne or steak and kidney pie. This is a Tolly Cobbold pub, serving real ales, and draught cider is available. There is a well-equipped children's play area outside. Well-behaved dogs on leads are welcome.

Telephone: 0473 830327.

How to get there: The Sorrel Horse is about 5 miles north of Ipswich. Leave the A14 Cambridge to Felixstowe road at the junction signed for Great Blakenham and Claydon. Do not take the B1113 but follow the minor road to Claydon. Go through the village and continue northwards along Norwich Road towards Barham and Coddenham. About 1 mile from Claydon, and immediately after the turning on the right to Coddenham, the Sorrel Horse is just off the road on the left behind a high hedge and opposite the main entrance to Shrubland Park.

Parking: There is plenty of parking at the Sorrel Horse.

Length of the walk: 4 miles. Maps: OS Landranger 155 Bury St Edmunds and Sudbury, 156 Saxmundham, Aldeburgh and surrounding area (GR 126514).

From the Sorrel Horse the walk soon enters Shrubland Park. The path climbs steadily, passing between the mansion and the stables, and then across several fields to the park gate. After that the walk goes through woods and fields and a leafy green lane to the hamlet of Barham Green, where fine houses flank a wide grassy common.

The return is past Barham church, which contains a statue by one of Britain's finest sculptors, Henry Moore, and then along a fairly level track on a hillside with wide views across the Gipping valley.

The Walk

Leave the Sorrel Horse and go left along the little-used road. Pass, on the right, a tiny collection of cottages known as Sharpstone Street, though there is no street other than the one you are on, and Old Smiths Cottage. Fifty yards after passing, on the left, the entrance to Spinney Cottage, leave the road, going right over a stile into woodland.

Walk between fences at first, then continue along a track through the woodland to emerge in open parkland by a clump of silver birches and a horse chestnut. Go leftish across a corner of the parkland towards a broad gap in the woodland on your left. Continue through light woodland, bearing right to pass, on your right, a deepish pit at the edge of the woodland. Swing round the end of the pit and again come out into the park.

Close by on your left are the massive green iron gates of Shrubland Hall. This large mansion, enhanced by Sir Charles Barry in the Italianate style around 1850, is now a health clinic. Go across the park, to the left of an enormous beech tree, aiming roughly towards three Scots pines on the far side. You are now heading towards the low, timber-built Russian Lodge, built as a pleasant place to take afternoon tea when that meal was introduced in the latter half of the 19th century, the evening meal beginning then to be taken later than previously.

By Russian Lodge join the drive, going left along it for 10 yards, passing the lodge on your right. Immediately swing right off the drive up through a few mature trees, climbing to the left corner of the white brick stable block on the crest of the hill. On your left you have a good view of Shrubland Hall. Cross the drive that leads into the stable courtyard and continue on the same line as before, with a hedge on your right, an open field and mature trees on your left.

Go over a wooden two-step stile in the wire fence and see in the distance the clay-tiled roof and the white and timbered gable end of one of Shrubland Park's gate lodges. Head for a few very tall oaks to the left of the lodge and there join a drive. Go right along the drive and leave the park by gate No 7.

Cross straight over the road, Sandy Hill, and take the main track towards Molecatchers Cottage and Oakwood Cottage. Where it divides, go left along a shingly drive, and through a wooden farm gate into the garden of Molecatchers Cottage. In 10 yards go right over a wooden stile beside farm gates, into a meadow.

As you follow the woods and fence on your right to the corner you can see, half-left, Hemingstone church. Go through the gap in the corner, where there is a two-step stile, and now follow the hedge on your left to the corner. Turn right, still with the hedge on your left, and walk to the next corner and then go diagonally half-left to the far corner by the woodland.

Leave the field by a stile next to a farm gate and in 20 yards walk through a belt of trees for 30 yards. Keep more or less straight on along a green lane, woods on the left, curving slightly to the left as you go. The green lane leads on through another woodland belt to emerge in a very big field, with, a long way off and half-right, the chimney of the Claydon cement works.

Go left for 50 yards to the point where the hedge on your left goes left. Here turn right across the field towards the house at Skeets Green, and pass it on your right. Bear left into a green lane and follow it all the way out to the road, which you meet at a T-junction.

By the junction there is a pink-washed, thatched cottage called North Corner which bears a 1920 Sun fire plate, dating from the days when insurance firms ran their own fire services and only attended fires at houses insured with them.

Go right along the road, in the direction marked Claydon and Ipswich, and follow this quiet, winding lane for nigh on a mile. You will pass Barham Manor, with its brick pillars and yew hedges, its star-topped Tudor chimneys and stepped gables. When you reach the church of St Mary and St Peter, take time to go inside and see Henry Moore's *Madonna and Child*, a memorial to the four men of Claydon who were killed in the Second World War. Originally in Claydon church,

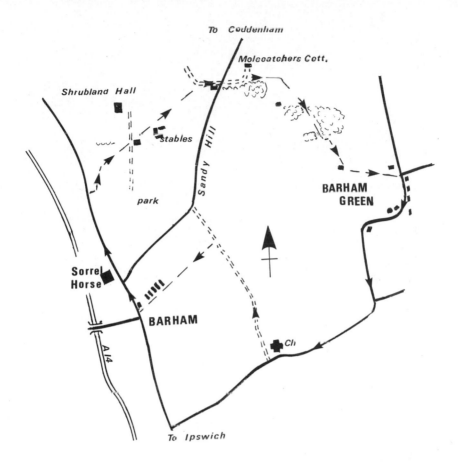

it was moved to St Mary's, Barham when St Peter's, Claydon was made redundant in 1975. Henry Moore himself was present to oversee the move. Before the statue was finally lowered to its new site it was placed upon sugar lumps, enabling minor adjustments to be made. Then the sugar was sprayed with water and the lumps dissolved. The statue settled down perfectly.

Turn right at the end of the churchyard on the bridleway to Coddenham Road. Follow this sandy track for ½ mile, with extensive views over the Gipping valley. After a bit, Shrubland Hall becomes visible ahead among the trees of Shrubland Park. Carry on down the hill, passing the gravel pits, till you reach a field on the left. Turn left immediately before the field and walk down between fields. Later pass chicken houses on the right and go out to the road. Turn right and walk back to the Sorrel Horse.

15 Debenham
The Red Lion

Debenham is a large, but compact, village in the middle of the county, and is the centre for a big rural community. It lies about 3 miles from the source of the river Deben, which flows through the village and south-eastward across Suffolk, past Woodbridge into the tidal estuary to join the sea between Felixstowe Ferry and Bawdsey.

There has been a Red Lion pub here since before 1600. It is a friendly pub, with two bars. On cold days a large wood fire crackles in the huge fireplace. The food is good and plentiful. Such mouth-watering dishes as tournedos Rossini, fillet steak stuffed with oysters cooked in butter and in a Madeira sauce, peppered sirloin steak and smoked trout are on the wide menu, together with children's meals. Real ale is served, including Ind Coope Burton Ale and Flowers IPA. Taunton Red Rock draught cider is also sold. Well-behaved dogs on leads are welcome.

Telephone: 0728 860113.

How to get there: Debenham is about 14 miles north of Ipswich, on the B1077, Eye road. From the east or west take the A1120, Stowmarket–Yoxford road and turn on to the B1077: The public car park and the Red Lion are both on the main road, close to the centre of the village.

Parking: There is a public car park near the southern end of the village, just by the church and the butcher's.

Length of the walk: 4 miles. Map: OS Landranger 156 Saxmundham, Aldeburgh and surrounding area (GR 173633).

The walk climbs a little up to a plateau above the village then circles along pretty green lanes, over towards Ashfield, before descending again, with views over to Winston, into Debenham.

The Walk

From the Red Lion, cross the road and go left for a few yards, and then turn right down Water Lane. This is sometimes awash; if so, go about 20 yards further north, over a bridge, and then turn back on yourself, but now alongside the houses, and then left to get to Water Lane, on the footway high above the water.

Continue along Water Lane to a road junction. Do not go right into Priory Lane, but left a little and on between hedges. In 20 yards go left on a rising cart track. Climb, with the hedge on the right, to the top, where the hedge ends. Go right on a grassy path, with the ditch on the right. Go through a gap in the cross-hedge and immediately turn left, with the hedge on the left. Go through the cross-hedge and continue on the grassy path, with the hedge on the left. Meet a road

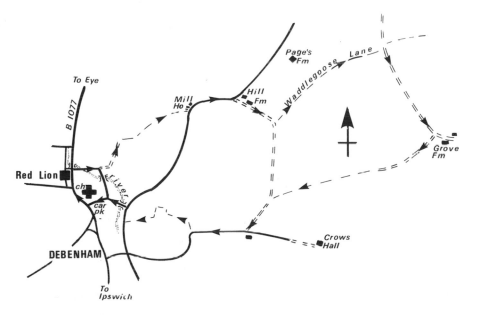

at a bend, with Mill House on your left, and go left along the road past this cluster of cottages.

When the road bends left, just before a brick farmhouse, go right, off the road, between farm buildings with barns on your left. Go along a farm track, with hedges on both sides. At a fork go left into a green lane, narrower than the lane you have been in.

After ½ mile you will reach a T-junction where there is a small clearing. Ahead over the fields, you may see Ashfield church. Turn right on a cart track, at first with hedges both sides, but later with an open field on the left and a ditch and a few isolated trees on the right. Ahead is a big farm.

When you get close to Grove Farm, turn off the track which leads to the farm, and go right along another cart track for about ½ mile. On the way, the path passes through a shelter belt. Presently it curves left and joins a farm track that has come in from the right. Soon join at an angle, by a half-timbered cottage, the drive that leads from Crows Hall. Turn right and walk towards Debenham. Winston church can be seen on the skyline to your left across the Deben valley.

Where the road swings left and downhill, you leave the road and go right with a hedge on your right. Follow the field edge, round a dog-leg, down the hill, left at the bottom corner of the field, and on till you come to a stile in the hedge on your right, and go through the hedge-line. Continue down the hill on a raised bank between fields, to join the road by a fenceless stile and a footpath signpost.

Turn right along the road to the road junction. Go left over the brick road bridge and walk back to Debenham. Turn right by the church and continue up the main street to the Red Lion.

16 Stutton
The King's Head

Stutton is a picturesque village overlooking Holbrook Bay, on the northern shore of the estuary of the river Stour. At the edge of the village is The Royal Hospital School, an independent mixed boarding school, originally for the children of those who serve, or have served, in the Royal or Merchant Navy. The buildings, with the playing fields sweeping down to the water's edge, form a prominent and very attractive landmark in the area.

The King's Head was built in the late 14th century and has long been a public house. There are plenty of old beams, nooks and crannies, and changes of floor level. A collection of old clay pipes is featured, as well as several ships in bottles. It is a popular, welcoming pub with a friendly staff, and is well known in the area for specialising in fresh fish of various kinds, served with chips. But the menu is much wider and includes lasagne, home-made steak and kidney pie, battered garlic chicken, moussaka, vegetarian dishes, and, to get the digestive juices working, let us mention one dish from the chargrill menu, 'King's Grill – a groaning platter of succulent rump steak, pork chop, sausage, egg, tomato, onion rings, french fries and petit pois'. Draught ales such as

67

Adnams IPA and guest beers are available. So is Dry Blackthorn draught cider. There is a garden area for children. Dogs are not allowed in the pub.

Telephone: 0473 328344.

How to get there: Stutton is south of Ipswich and is on the B1080, between Brantham (A137) and Holbrook.

Parking: There is plenty of parking at the pub.

Length of the walk: 5 miles. Map: OS Landranger 169 Ipswich and The Naze area (GR 148348).

This walk follows a country lane to the Stour estuary at Stutton Ness, where the river Stour, which for most of its length forms the boundary between Suffolk and Essex, is about a mile wide, and sea birds abound. Further downstream, amid the towering cranes and busy shipping of Harwich, Parkeston and Felixstowe, is the confluence of the rivers Stour and Orwell.

The route continues along the river bank for about 2 miles, almost to Stutton Mill, a lonely and delightful old pink-washed house set at the water's edge, overlooking the estuary. The return is along quiet tree-lined lanes.

The Walk

From the King's Head, go to the bus shelter, cross the road and take a narrow path, between two houses, which leads out to a broad lawn. Keep beside the hedge and at the corner zig-zag right and left through the hedge, and continue with the hedge now on the left. At the end go right along a broad, well-used path and when you reach a tarmac lane turn left, passing a pair of white-painted cottages on the right. Where the surfaced track swings left to a large house, go straight forward on a gravel farm track which soon passes some old weather-boarded barns on the left.

Keep on the wide lane, edged with mature trees, till you reach the river bank where the track makes a sharp right turn. At this point you can look straight down the river across Holbrook Bay. Keep on the track, which runs parallel to the shore, and in about ¼ mile reach Stutton Ness.

Make your way out on to the sand at the Ness where there is an excellent view of the whole Stour estuary. Upstream is Manningtree, and Mistley with its quay, and downstream you can see Parkeston Quay and Harwich, whilst beyond are the massive container-handling cranes of Felixstowe towering above the ships. Looking inland across Holbrook Bay, you can see the tower of the Royal Hospital School.

The track you were following soon ends in a shallow gravel pit.

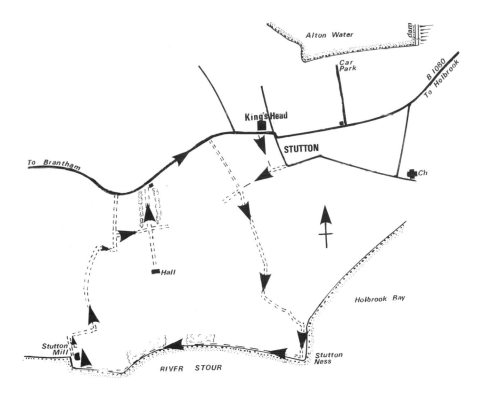

Here keep straight on along the edge of a field at the top of a small gravel cliff which forms the river bank. At the end of the field you come to a tree-girt, grassy clearing. Cross the field and you will enter mixed oak and sweet chestnut woodlands, on a narrow path close to the top of the river cliff. Follow the path across another field and into woodlands again, but here your path is a wider, grassy one.

At the next narrow clearing in the wood, find and cross a plank bridge into oak woods and make your way left to walk along the top of the river bank. This soon leads into the corner of a large field. Keep on the edge, still beside the estuary. At the corner of the field pass the end of a shelter belt of conifers, and, immediately after, turn right along the permissive footpath, passing a paddock on the left, with the pink-washed Stutton Mill behind. Go through the hedge at the end and, leaving the shelter belt, turn left. When you reach the wall of Stutton Mill turn right and follow the side of the marvellous garden, out to the surfaced drive.

Turn right along the drive, which soon makes a sharp turn to the left, and in nearly ½ mile pass the white Queech Farm on the left. The road makes a sharp right and left turn. Shortly after passing a red-brick cottage on the right, turn right along a rough gravel track with a hedge on the right.

When you reach a drive at right angles, you will see, on the right, Stutton Park at the end of the drive. Here, turn left and follow the drive straight out to the road beside the park lodge. Turn right along the road towards Stutton. You will reach the King's Head in about ¾ mile.

Other local attractions: Close by Stutton is Alton Water, a 2½ mile long lake, with public parking and many leisure activities, such as sailing, board-sailing, fishing and watching the lake's birds. The entrance is on the road from Stutton to Holbrook, about ¼ mile east of the pub.

Bedfield
The Crown

Bedfield is a small village comprising several hamlets and isolated farms, stretching about 2 miles from Little Green in the south to Long Green in the north. This area is part of the plateau known as High Suffolk, and is intensively cultivated, mainly with arable crops.

The Crown, a traditional English village pub, is in the centre of the parish, and lies in a cul-de-sac that leads to moated, late 16th century Bedfield Hall and the adjacent church of St Nicholas. This unspoilt, thatched inn has been here since 1780. It is off the beaten track for many people, but is well worth seeking out. Besides good ales and mostly home-made food there are many bar games and amusements, and tables outside for summer eating and drinking. Such meals as lasagne, chilli con carne, scampi, and a dish called the Crown Fry-up are on offer. A wide range of puddings is listed too, including gooey chocolate cake and home-cooked apple pie. No meals are served on Tuesdays. The landlord serves Greene King and Marstons ales, and brings in guest ales from the small local and little-known breweries which produce excellent beer. Children are well catered for. There is a large play area with a climbing frame, though as the area is open to the road the smaller ones will need watching. Dogs on leads are welcome.

Telephone: 0728 628431.

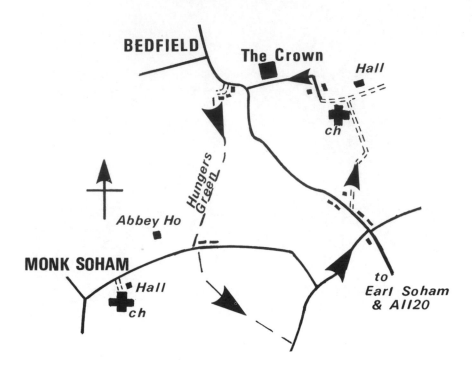

How to get there: Bedfield is 3 miles north of Earl Soham. From the A1120 Stowmarket to Yoxford road, turn north on a minor road at the eastern end of Earl Soham village to reach Bedfield. At Bedfield turn right along the road to the church for 100 yards to reach the Crown.

Parking: There is a car park at the Crown.

Length of the walk: 3 miles. Map: OS Landranger 156 Saxmundham, Aldeburgh and surrounding area (GR 223665).

From the Crown the walk goes south to Monk Soham along a common called Hungers Green, where meadow plants abound. The path leads across three fields, all characteristic of the arable farming in this part of Suffolk. You return by way of a leafy green lane to Bedfield church and the moated hall.

The Walk

From the Crown walk westward, back along the road to the T-junction, and turn right. Pass a small pond on the left and in 200 yards turn left on to a short narrow road, to pass Anvil Cottage at a bend.

The road ends at White House Farm. Continue on a wide grass path with a pond on the right and swing left on the path into a long narrow field. At the end go through a gate and enter a short lane which leads out into Hungers Green, an unspoilt meadow. Follow the hedge on the left which eventually leads, through a lane, to the road.

Turn left on the road and in about 50 yards cross the ditch on the right at a footpath sign. Head across the field and, at the far side, cross the boundary into the next field, very close to the corner of that field. Swing right for a few yards to the corner and, keeping in the same general direction as before, continue on a wide, grassy headland, making for the right-hand end of a line of trees ahead. You will find that the trees form a thick hedge.

Pass the end of this hedge and cross a concrete culvert. Keep a hedge on your left, but when it ends bear slightly left up the hill to a gap in a hedge at the top. Here you join a grassy headland farm track and follow it, with the hedge on the left, to a short left-right dog-leg out to the road.

Turn left and walk along the road. In ¼ mile, at a T-junction keep straight on, and in another ¼ mile, turn left at a crossroads.

In 100 yards and just after a white house on the right, turn right along a broad, grassy, green lane signed 'Public Bridleway to Tannington 1¾ miles'. Keep on the lane, which leads towards Bedfield Hall, an attractive pink-painted farmhouse, 4 bays wide, and with gables at each end. Before reaching the hall turn off the lane through the churchyard of St Nicholas. If you have time to visit the church, you will find an unusual font cover, over 6 ft high. Go through the churchyard and out to the road on the far side. Walk along the road, which, after swinging round to the left, reaches, in ¼ mile, the Crown.

18 Grundisburgh
The Dog

Grundisburgh is a thriving village, equidistant from Ipswich and Woodbridge, with a great sense of community. The green, between the church and the pub, is a focal point for the village. Here the shoppers exchange pleasantries and the young people of the village gossip and banter in the evenings and at weekends. The river Lark runs through the village and across the green.

The 17th century Dog inn has a warm, mellow atmosphere, enhanced by settles and furniture of old oak. It is an Ind Coope house. Such real ales as Benskins, Burton IPA and Tetley are available, as well as Old English draught cider. There is an imaginative, mouth-watering menu. The pub specialises in home-made pies, such as venison, steak and Guinness, and chicken and asparagus. Such dishes as prawn-filled trout, spicy chicken, spiced lamb and swordfish are also on offer. Children having a meal with their parents are welcome but there is no garden area outside. Lunches are served every day between 12 noon and 2 pm and evening meals between 7 pm and 9.30 pm (but not on Sundays). Dogs are allowed in the public bar.

Telephone: 0473 735267.

How to get there: Grundisburgh is 3 miles north-west of Woodbridge and reached from the B1079. The Dog is in the centre of the village, near the green.

Parking: The Dog has a car park at the rear. There is also ample street-side parking in the vicinity of the pub and the green.

Length of the walk: 3½ miles. Map: OS Landranger 156 Saxmundham, Aldeburgh and surrounding area (GR 224510).

This walk goes up the valley of the Lark, climbs a hill with views of Burgh's windmill and drops down to the edge of Hasketon parish, returning beside meadows with a view of Burgh House.

The Walk

From the Dog, cross the road and go half-left past the bus shelter, over the green towards the church. Go right along the road in front of the church, over the raised walkway beside the ford and on to meet the main road again.

On the left pass a large, timber-framed house called Basts. It was built in the early 1500s by a London salt merchant, John Wall. His son Thomas, also a salt merchant, has a nearby close named after him. On the corner post of Basts is carved a salt cellar, and more are in the stonework of the church roof. Continue round and, just after passing Gurdon Road on the right, go left along a wide earth farm track between fences.

Cross the stream by a footbridge beside the ford and continue to the end of the track. Go over the stile beside the red metal gate, and on with the hedge on your right. At the barbed wire cross-fence go over the stile and on to the corner of the field. In the corner go over the two-bar wooden stile into a small, narrow field, and keep straight on. Just before the next cross-hedge, almost under the grid lines, go left over a two-bar stile and immediately right and walk 3 yards out to the field edge. Continue with the hedge on the right. Go over a cross-ditch by a culvert and, in 50 yards, bear right over a footbridge over the Lark and go right.

In the next section you will see two churches. Burgh the nearer and Clopton the other. They are only about ¼ mile apart.

Cut across the corner of the field to the next hedge corner and follow that hedge to the metal gate onto the road by Manor Farm. Go right, under the grid lines, up to the top of the hill and down the other side as far as a farm track on the left by the house Finn Haugh. Leave the road here and climb the track. Keep on past a house, an old cart

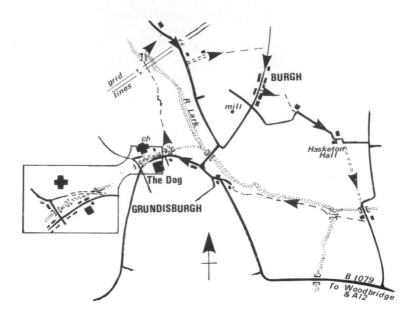

lodge and some barns till you reach an internal corner of a big field.

Across the field you will see a line of electricity poles. Go towards the big double pole and walk parallel to the line of poles and to the right of them. Down in the valley bottom find a dilapidated brick culvert and go over the stream. Continue following the poles to the far side where you walk out to the road by another double pole.

Go right along the road to the village of Burgh. Note the small, round, thatched house on the left. After passing Dunedin on the right, and just before the bungalow Ashlea on the left, go left off the road, walking between fences for 50 yards into a field.

Continue in the same direction, and when the hedge on the left ends keep straight on across the field to meet the side of a wood. At the wood go rightish and follow the edge of the wood on the left, out to meet a road by a right-angle bend, with Lea Cottage on your left.

Keep straight on along the road, going round bends to pass Hasketon Hall on the right. Take care to listen out for vehicles and watch children. At the left-hand bend, where the road goes uphill between banks, leave the road by going straight ahead with high trees on the right. Follow the grassy track until you meet a road at a bend. Go straight ahead, pass a cottage, cross a bridge and, opposite Bridge Cottage on the left, go right along a grassy track, with trees and a river on your right.

76

Later cross the river by an elegant footbridge. Pass through a cross-hedge and keep on, always with the stream on your right. The path meanders a little through scrub. Go over a stile into a minuscule field, then over another stile into a long field. Burgh House is away on your right. Near the far end of this field go over a two-step stile on the left, up a bank, and turn right along the headland path. By some cupressus, join a drive, pass Vine Cottage and walk out to the road in Grundisburgh.

Turn right, and, after passing Half Moon Lane, in 100 yards keep left to follow the main road, curving left all the time, to return to the Dog.

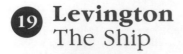

19 Levington
The Ship

Levington, a small village beside the lonely marshes which fringe this part of the river Orwell, is probably better known to yachtsmen than to the general public. The area must have been known, too, to Scandinavian warriors as, in 1904, the remains of a Viking ship were found in the mud here. The crag, a sandy, shelly subsoil, abundant hereabouts, was found, in 1718, to be an excellent fertilizer. It contains nodules of coprolite, and its use was discovered by an ancestor of the Fison family, the founders of the firm which still deals in fertilizers.

The Ship inn on Gun Hill dates back to the 14th century. It is reputed to have been a hideout of Margaret Catchpole, who was born near here and whose exploits connected with smuggling are well recorded. It has a fine reputation in the county, both for its friendly atmosphere and for its well-kept ales and good cooking.

All the food, which is served from 12 noon till 2 pm seven days a week, is home-made and the menu is changed daily. An abiding favourite is steak and kidney pie. A broad spectrum of ales can be had here, including Greene King, Tolly Cobbold, Burton, Flowers, Tetley and Wethereds, as well as Dry Blackthorn cider. On warm days the tables in front of the inn are full. There is a garden area for children, but dogs are best left elsewhere.

Telephone: 0473 659573.

How to get there: Levington lies halfway along the east side of the Orwell estuary and is 7 miles from Ipswich. From the south and west take the A14 main road towards Felixstowe, and from the north-east take the A12 towards Colchester. At the junction between the A12 (from Lowestoft) and the A14 go towards Felixstowe on the A14. Two miles beyond the junction turn right carefully off the dual-carriageway on to a minor road and in a mile turn left. In the village keep left. The Ship is a few yards beyond the church.

Parking: There is a large car park behind the pub.

Length of the walk: 4½ miles. Map: OS Landranger 169 Ipswich and The Naze area (GR 235390).

Allow extra time for this walk as there is a temptation to dawdle while watching the river, its traffic and its wildlife. At first the route is along the Orwell estuary, and from the higher land near the Ship a wide stretch of the river reaching down to its mouth between Harwich and Felixstowe is visible. Ipswich, too, is a port. Cargo and container ships sail up and down the Orwell daily, twisting and turning round the navigation buoys which mark the deep water channel.

The walk passes the Levington Yacht Harbour where the smaller boats, motor and sailing cruisers that use the Suffolk rivers for recreation and leisure activities can berth. Whilst it is fascinating in summer to see the variety of craft on the river, perhaps the best time to walk the area is in the winter when the small boats have been laid up. In those times there is solitude on the banks of the Orwell, the occasional walker sharing this wide expanse with the large number of ducks, geese and other river birds that visit the east coast estuaries.

The route returns inland, passing a large riding establishment and a national horticultural research station.

The Walk

Take the footpath opposite the Ship, at the right-hand side of the orange colour-washed thatched cottage. This path shortly leads into the corner of a field where you have a magnificent panoramic view of the Orwell estuary with, in the distance, the huge cranes of the port of Felixstowe. You can see the great container vessels and the passenger and car ferries which ply across the North Sea to Belgium, Holland and Denmark. Walk down towards the left-hand distant crane, and at the other side of the field, tunnel through a blackthorn thicket to the river wall. Here turn left towards the head of Levington Creek.

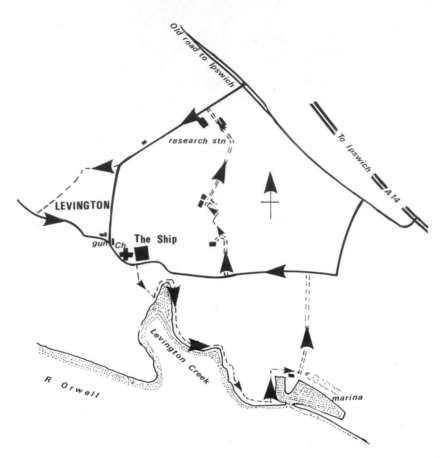

Round the head of the creek where several houseboats are moored and keep on the river wall. You will pass a lagoon on the left which is a sanctuary for winter wading birds. The Suffolk Wildlife Trust and the Suffolk Ornithologists Group have placed a notice describing the reserve. A little further along the river wall, you will pass a series of flat beds where silt dredged from the Levington Yacht Harbour has been pumped to dry out. On reaching the edge of the marina, turn to the left and make your way alongside the boat park. At the shoreward end, turn right and go past some sheds to the point where the harbour access road enters the site.

Turn left along the access road for ½ mile, shortly passing Stratton Hall Woods, and reach the public road at a T-junction. Turn left and in 200 yards pass, on the left, the entrance to Stratton Hall, noting the horses' heads on the iron gates.

After passing two pairs of cottages on the right, walk a further 150 yards and turn right up a track leading to Levington Hall. Where it makes a wide sweep round to the left towards the house, go straight on, keeping close to the edge of the lawn. Pass through a narrow tree belt, over a stile into a paddock. Follow the field boundary on the right and at the corner go over another stile and turn left on a sandy track leading towards a farmhouse. At the farm turn right on a tarmac farm road and continue on the narrow private road which leads through the research station. Pass a weather station on the left and then some buildings on the right. Go out to the road and turn left.

Keep on the road for ¼ mile to pass the very attractive White House Farm on the right and in a further ¼ mile, at the edge of the village, just before the first house on the right and under two electricity power lines, leave the road. Join the bridleway on the right which immediately bears left to follow a high hedge on the left. Shortly the path veers to the right down a hill, through a hedge and out to the corner of a field. Continue on a headland path, with the hedge on the right, which will lead you in ¼ mile to a road.

Turn left and climb the hill to Levington village. At the village sign keep right by an old cannon underneath a crab apple tree. You will shortly pass the church and in a few yards return to the Ship.

20 Mendham
The Sir Alfred Munnings

On the banks of the river Waveney, at the northern boundary of the county, lies the tiny village of Mendham. Here a bridge over the river carries a minor road leading to Harleston and about ¼ mile downstream, beside the river, is Mendham Mill. The Mill House was the birthplace of Sir Alfred Munnings RA, the painter. The centenary of his birth is commemorated by the village sign, depicting a woman leading a horse, a reminder of one of Munnings' paintings. The land to the east of the village is a low plateau of mainly arable farmland which falls in a steep bank down to the river valley where watermeadows are criss-crossed with drainage ditches.

Mendham's famous artist son is remembered again in the Sir Alfred Munnings country hotel and restaurant which is situated in the centre of the village opposite the church. It is said that the artist often set up his easel nearby. The inn is an attractive cream-washed, two-storey building, formerly a dwelling. Unusually, there is, at the southern end, a small room which provides the village post office. The large carpeted bar area is very pleasantly furnished. Ranged against the wall are lavishly upholstered, comfortable bench seats and the room is well decorated with pictures including prints of Munnings' works.

The fare at the bar is reasonably priced and there is much to choose from, including eight different fillings for jacket potatoes. Delicious soup comes in generous bowls. Omelette and chips, ham, egg and chips, home-made curry and rice are just some of the dishes on the menu. A children's menu is available. With prior notice, meals can be provided for diabetics. The well-appointed restaurant serves lunches and dinners with a wide-ranging and interesting menu. Adnams real ale is on sale. Adnams Southwold bitters are made from East Anglian malt and old Kentish hop varieties with the delightful names of Fuggles and Goldings, making a refreshingly hoppy bitter. Old English draught cider is also available. Well-behaved dogs on leads are welcome.

Telephone: 0379 852358.

How to get there: Mendham is 4 miles due east of Harleston. From the A143 road, which runs between Bury St Edmunds, Diss and Great Yarmouth, turn off at a minor road on the Harleston bypass, to reach Mendham in 3 miles.

Parking: There is a car park at the rear of the hotel, but for the walk use the village car park opposite the post office.

Length of the walk: 5 miles. Map: OS Landranger 156 Saxmundham, Aldeburgh and surrounding area (GR 270829).

From the village the walk leads uphill, away from the river, to make a broad sweep across mixed pasture and arable fields, with wide views of the area. About halfway round the circuit, you walk down a delightful, narrow, leafy and sunken road with a little stream alongside, expressively named Hollow Lane, which leads to the hamlet of Withersdale Street. The return is across Mendham Marshes, an extensive tract of watermeadows, to the bank of the Waveney river and thence to All Saints church.

The Walk

From the Sir Alfred Munnings pub, walk round the corner, past the post office and on to the crossroads. Go straight over, climb the hill and walk as far as Rose Cottage and the footpath sign on the left.

Turn left along the track to cream-coloured Rose Cottage. Just after the cross-hedge on the right, go through a black metal gate and cross the meadow diagonally, under the electricity wires, to leave by a black pedestrian gate near a shed. Cross a small area to another black wooden gate to emerge in the corner of a field. Walk with the hedge on the left, with wide views north across the

Waveney valley.

Leave the field to enter a short track with a pond on the right. Turn left through a pair of wooden gates and walk diagonally across this field, heading to the right of the farmhouse, Walsham Hall. At the far side cross a footbridge to join a road on a bend.

Go right along the road, passing Oakhill Farm on the right and Laurel Farm on the left. About 200 yards after Laurel Farm leave the road, going right, into a field. Follow the field edge, with the hedge on the left. At the end corner, cross a ditch and go left a yard or so, then continue in the same direction as before, with the hedge on the left. At the end of the next field, go through a metal farm gate. Now curve in a quarter circle arc to meet the farm drive just south of Moat Farm.

Walk along the drive to join Mundy's Road. Go right for 20 yards and then left off the road, over a culvert. Cross this field, bearing right diagonally to a prominent oak at the end of a hedge. Go ahead, veering a little to the left to walk roughly towards a house you can see in the distance. If there is a field division fence here, keep it on your right. Your direction across this field is in line with the hedge you have just left. At the far side cross the next ditch by a plank bridge, and continue in the same direction with the hedge and ditch on your right. At the end of this field you will meet a hard farm track at a bend. Keep straight on, on the farm track, till you meet a road, Foxes Lane, by a house and a wartime pill-box.

Cross straight over into Hollow Lane, and walk until you get to within a yard or so of the end, near a T-junction with the Metfield road. Turn right off the road through an elderly metal gate into a long thin field. At the far end of this field go over another geriatric gate. With the fence on the left, go to the last metal gate, which takes you out to the Withersdale road.

Turn left, pass the handsome red-brick Georgian house, and at the T-junction turn right by the grassy triangle. Walk through the village, with care as there is no footway in places. At the T-junction in ½ mile, go right and very shortly round the bend to the left, by Priory Farm.

In about 100 more yards leave the road, going right along a wide farm track, with farm buildings on your left and a fence on your right. The track then runs through a 15 yard wide enclosure with fences on both sides, for almost ¼ mile. At the end of the broad drift way, turn right into a narrower grass track with fences on both sides and a deep ditch on the left. The track swings right a little and then, still following the ditch on the left, turns sharp left and in 50 yards ends at a gate to a large field.

Enter the field and bear right towards Mendham church. At the far

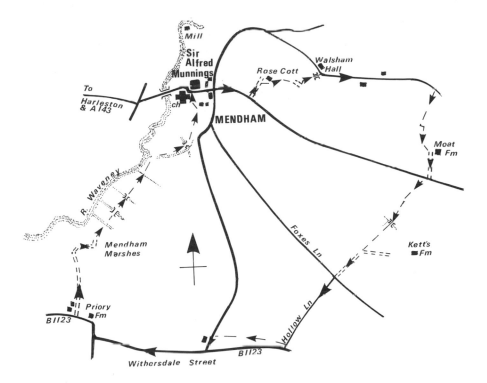

side of the field come to a deep ditch. If the bridge, damaged by floods, has not been replaced, turn right and follow the ditch to its end, returning on the opposite bank. Continue in the same direction towards the church and cross the next drainage channel by a sleeper cart bridge. At the next field boundary cross a stile followed by a footbridge.

You now have the river Waveney about 50 yards to the left. Keep on in the same direction, crossing a small ditch by a culvert, and after that keep close to the river bank. Where the river bends sharply left, go through a gate and turn right, away from the river, following a ditch on the right.

After passing the ends of two ditches running at right angles to your route, you come to a substantial sleeper cart bridge across a wide ditch, and enter another field. Here keep on, following a fence and small ditch on the right, through a gateway into a broader meadow at the edge of the village. Go slightly right towards the nearest corner of a barn on the far side of the field, and, about 30 yards before the barn, swing left to a stile in a corner of the field close to the church. Cross the stile and go to the churchyard gate and turn right, back to the starting point.

21 Easton
The White Horse

Easton lies on the north side of the narrow, tranquil river Deben which flows down to Woodbridge, where it discharges into a great tidal estuary. Visitors to Easton will find in this small, quiet and compact village a degree of similarity among the older houses and cottages. This is because in the last century the land at Easton was owned by the Dukes of Hamilton, who built houses for the estate staff, among which are three circular thatched cottages with half-moon dormer windows and a large central brick chimney. These round buildings have a fairy tale air about them.

At the centre of the village stands a triangular grassy green and, on one side, the White Horse sits snugly among a row of dwellings. Built around 1600, it has the flavour of a cottage outside, but once inside the pub, it is seen to be spacious. There is a comfortable bar area, a pleasant restaurant and a family dining-room where parents and children can enjoy their bar meals. The premises have recently been renovated and tastefully furnished with antique pine furniture in keeping with the building. It was rather a surpise to find in the bar area a full size wooden lectern, formerly in a church in Leicester. We wonder if it is used by the scorer at the local darts match, or perhaps

Easton residents are given to making speeches from time to time.

The landlord, who at one time was a chef at Buckingham Palace, cooks the meals. He offers an interesting range of fare and the menu is changed daily. Culinary delights such as Scotch sirloin steak with traditional pepper sauce, roast fillet of lamb with rosemary and garlic, and (superb) délice of salmon with champagne sauce are served. Among the range of beers, Tolly Cobbold real ale is available and you can have Dry Blackthorn draught cider. The garden at the rear is equipped with a variety of exciting play apparatus for children. Well-behaved dogs on leads are welcome.

Telephone: 0728 746456.

How to get there: Easton is about 2 miles north of Wickham Market and can be reached by turning off the B1116 (Framlingham–Wickham Market road). The White Horse is in the centre of the village, close to the church.

Parking: The car park is on the opposite side of the road to the pub.

Length of the walk: 3½ miles. Map: OS Landranger 156 Saxundham, Aldeburgh and surrounding area (GR 284587).

A short walk encircling this unspoilt village. The route goes across farmland to the river Deben and back, taking in the ruins of a 12th century priory – Letheringham Abbey – Letheringham Watermill in its attractive setting, and later passing the kennels of the Easton Harriers.

The Walk

From the White Horse turn left, away from the church, and go along the road for 100 yards, turning left up a track between Lavender Cottage and Pedlars Halt which leads to the Easton Cricket Club. Pass the cricket ground on the right and follow the crinkle-crankle wall on the left to the far left corner of a big field, with Maids Wood ahead and Park Cottage away on your right.

The park used to be completely surrounded by a crinkle-crankle wall, that is a wall which swings in and out in a series of regular circular arcs, designed to give extra strength whilst using fewer bricks than a straight nine-inch deep garden wall. Alas it was not strong enough to withstand the ravages of age and tree root growth and although there is much left, the wall has, in several places, tumbled down.

Go through to the left into the corner of another field, and again continue with Easton Park and its wall on your left. Later cross a culvert into another field and at the next, rounded, corner find a two-

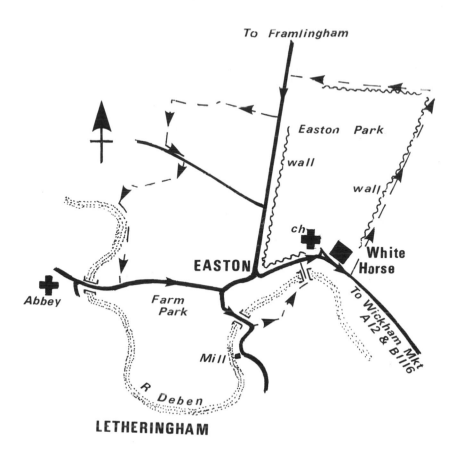

To Framlingham

Easton Park

wall

wall

ch

White Horse

EASTON

Abbey

Farm Park

To Wickham Mkt A12 & B1116

Mill

R Deben

LETHERINGHAM

sleeper footbridge and go into the next field. Continue, hedge on left, to join a road by another two-sleeper footbridge opposite a pair of cottages, and turn left. Walk for 300 yards on this quiet road, passing Martley Hall on the left and the thatched Old Kennels on the right. At the kennels look back to see the moulded plaster decoration above the archway.

Presently, at a very wide gap, go right into a field and proceed with a hedge on your right. Follow the curvy edge of this field, with hedge or woods on your right, for about ¼ mile, with Easton Farm Park away on your left. Go over a cross-stream by a sleeper footbridge and through a broad gap between two very substantial circular wooden posts.

Turn left, with the hedge on the left, climbing slightly, and eventually walk out to the road. Go left beside the road for 100 yards then walk up into the field on your right, and in 20 yards pick up a hedge on the right. After a while drop down into the rounded corner of this odd-shaped field and walk beside a stream which soon joins the river Deben. At the next corner go left away from the river for 10 yards then right a bit over a stile. Cross the field entrance and go over another stile. Walk between the hedge and the barbed wire fence and out to the road. At this point you could make a detour, by going right, to see Letheringham church and the abbey ruins.

Turn left and go along the road. Soon you will pass the farm complex of Easton Farm Park. The circular building on the far right of the complex, with a white turret on top, is the light and airy old dairy. Away on your left see two of the circular thatched cottages. At a grassy triangle turn right, and then in 50 yards go left. This is a low-lying road, occasionally, after very heavy rain, subject to flooding, and there are height indicators along the road. Cross the river Deben, and when the road bends to the right you go left on a shingle track.

From this junction you could detour to the right to see the white, weatherboarded Letheringham Watermill.

The shingly track leads to a cottage, Four Bridges. Opposite its wrought iron gate, turn left off the track across the greensward to a stile. Go over the stile and footbridge, on along a hedge-lined path, and over three more bridges. Just after crossing the much larger last bridge you will see on the right, at the kennels of the Easton Harriers, another of those round, thatched cottages. Walk out to the road opposite a handsome section of the crinkle-crankle wall and turn right along the road, back past the church to the White Horse.

Other local attractions: On the edge of the village is the Easton Farm Park (open daily) where visitors may encounter a wide range of farm animals and view, from a specially constructed gallery, the modern milking parlour in action. Next door to the pub is a craft shop.

22 Huntingfield
The Huntingfield Arms

Huntingfield is a small village, near Halesworth, with a tributary of the
river Blyth running through it. The Huntingfield Arms stands at a road
junction, facing the village green on which a large chestnut tree stands.
The pub was originally the house for the farm manager of
Heveningham Hall and the building dates from about 1810. The
central bar separates the restaurant area from the more informal area
to the right of the doorway. At the rear is a games area and overnight
accommodation is available.

Good home-cooked food is served at lunchtime and in the
evenings, every day, in the bar and in the restaurant. Dishes such as
tuna and pasta bake, steak and kidney pie and chips, chilli con carne
and salmon with fresh crab and salad are on the menu. The real ales
are Adnams, Charrington IPA and Worthington, and both Red Rock
and Dry Blackthorn draught cider are on offer. Tables and chairs are
set out in front for use on sunny days. The pub welcomes children,
but please leave your dogs outside.

Telephone: 0986 798320.

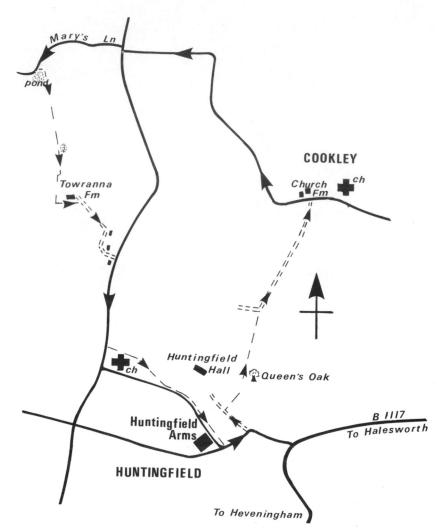

How to get there: Huntingfield is 4 miles south-west of Halesworth, and reached from the A144 south of the town. About 1½ miles west of Walpole on the B1117 Heveningham and Laxfield road, take the turning to Huntingfield which is ½ mile away. The pub is in the centre of the village.

Parking: There is a large car park behind the pub and there is some parking by the village hall on the opposite side of the green.

92

Length of the walk: 5 miles. Map: OS Landranger 156 Saxmundham, Aldeburgh and surrounding area (GR 341738).

This is an easy walk, although undulating at times and climbing to high ground on the way over to Cookley, from where there are fine views. Some of the route is beside arable land and some is through light woodland beside a stream. En route you will pass the Queen's Oak, which is one of the oldest oaks in England, and Huntingfield Hall with its lovely copper beeches.

The Walk

Leave the Huntingfield Arms and go east along the road, Bridge Street. The brick bridge is capped by an iron parapet made at the famous ironworks of Garrett and Son of Leiston. Although the foundry is no longer working, there is a museum on the site, at the old Longshop in Leiston.

Where the road swings round to the right go left on a shingly farm track, with poplars on your left. In 200 yards, just before the entrance to Huntingfield Hall, leave the track, going right up the hill with a hedge on the left. As you climb you will see Huntingfield Hall on your left. This has an interesting parapet on the south front, probably a later addition. It is conjectured that its unusual height of 10 ft, hiding the roof behind it, probably made the view of the house attractive from the Vanneck family's other property, Heveningham Hall. On the right you will pass the ancient Queen's Oak standing alone in the field. Oliver Rackham, an authority on the countryside, particularly trees and hedges, estimates it to be about 1,000 years old. You see it stag-headed today; it was also recorded as being stag-headed in 1780. The Queen referred to is probably Queen Elizabeth I, who had a cousin hereabouts.

Still climbing, pass through a cross-hedge by a culvert. When the land flattens out at the top you can see, half-right, the tower of Cookley church. Join a concrete track at a bend, and with wide views all round, carry on in the same direction as before. Now you have a hedge on your right and a field beyond that is Broomgreen Covert.

Meet the road at the bottom of the track opposite Church Farm, and go left along the road, until in about a mile your reach a staggered crossroads. Go straight ahead on the road signed to Linstead Magna. In about 300 yards the road swings to the right and continues in a slow bend round to the left for a further 300 yards. Then, where the road makes a sharp right turn, turn left off the road at a footpath sign.

Pass a small pond on the right and then head along a grassy strip between two arable fields, towards a white house in the distance. At the far side of the field keep the pond surrounded by trees on the left, and continue straight on with a ditch and hedge on the left. After passing on the left a sleeper footbridge across the ditch, the route of another footpath, keep straight on for a few yards and then go right and left to continue with the hedge on the left. At the corner of the field go over a sleeper bridge and go through a fence between two widely spaced wooden rails. Turn left and follow the well-trimmed hedge on the left to pass in front of Towranna Farm. Turn right along the gravel farm drive and, after passing a small stable and a bungalow, reach the road.

On the road turn right and walk for 400 yards down the hill to the bottom, where there are white rails on both sides. Turn left off the road over a two-plank footbridge into the corner of a long field. Follow its edge as the field narrows then widens again, to the end where you turn right, and keep bearing right through woodland. Eventually you come to a fence with a stile in it, and on its right is a footbridge.

If you wish to visit the church, turn right across the bridge and then right along the road for 200 yards. St Mary's has an amazingly colourful roof, painted by a former vicar's wife. It can be illuminated for your benefit. The font cover too is quite splendid.

To continue the walk, go past the bridge on your right and keep straight on, over a sandy, tree-rooty path through light woodland with a stream on the right. When you reach a concrete track go straight across it and continue along a leafy lane. On each side are big gnarly old trees.

At the end, by a footpath sign, you reach a road. Go right, over the bridge and back to the Huntingfield Arms.

23 Sweffling
The White Horse

The village of Sweffling is on the western slope of the shallow Alde valley, where the river meanders south to Snape. The Romans came to this part of Britain, and they built an east-west road just a bit further north. A bronze head of Emperor Claudius was found in the river Alde at Rendham, a village on the opposite bank of the Alde just north of Sweffling. The Suffolk poet George Crabbe, who was born in 1754, spent 13 years in this area when he was curate of Sweffling.

The White Horse inn is 200 years old. It has an interesting collection of old farming inplements, and other bygones, and is a friendly place where landlord and locals alike smile and make you welcome. On colder days, a log fire warms the bar, which has an unusual amusement for both adults and children. A large stag's head is mounted above the fireplace, with a hook in the stag's nose. A ring hangs from a string in the ceiling a yard or so away, and you swing the ring, aiming to get it on the hook.

Much of the food is home-made. There is soup, fish pie topped with grated cheese, lasagne, steak and mushroom pie, cheese and onion quiche, fresh grilled salmon cutlet, large English lamb chops, rump steak, and beef- or cheese-burgers with chips. The White Horse is a freehouse serving Adnams Southwold ales and Strongbow cider. Well-behaved dogs are welcome.

Telephone: 072 878 787.

How to get there: Sweffling's White Horse inn lies at a crossroads on the Saxmundham to Framlingham road (B1119), about 2 miles west of the A12.

Parking: There is ample parking by the White Horse.

Length of the walk: 2¾ miles. Map: OS Landranger 156 Saxmundham, Aldeburgh and surrounding area (GR 344643).

This short walk encompasses the twin villages of Sweffling and Rendham. These settlements are a mere ½ mile apart, but separated by the river Alde, which here is a narrow river, in contrast to its wide estuary downstream at Aldeburgh.

Once you have crossed the watermeadows, the walk is through Rendham and up the north side of the valley along headland paths to the river again. A field path leads to Sweffling church, and one returns to the White Horse on a path across meadow land which has been planted under the Countryside Commission's 'Countryside Premium Scheme' where the farmer has sown traditional meadow grasses over which the public may walk and children play.

The Walk

From the White Horse corner, take the road towards Saxmundham and in a few yards, where the road bends sharply right, go left down a short, grassy lane, through a kissing-gate and into the corner of a broad meadow. Cross this field and swing right to keep the shallow boundary ditch on the left. In the far corner go over a stile, cross the river Alde and follow a narrow path out to the road at Rendham.

Turn right along the road for 10 yards and then bear left up a slight hill, passing the old chapel with its iron railings. You will join a road from the right and almost immediately pass on the right a road and a large green triangle on which stands a lone oak. Go straight on. This road leads past Rendham Court on the left. At Hall Farm Road, keep straight on towards Peasenhall and when, in about 50 yards, the road swings left, go right and follow the field boundary on the right.

At the end of the field go over a two-sleeper footbridge and continue roughly in the same direction but now with a ditch on the left. At the next field boundary go over a culvert and then go left a few yards to follow a deep ditch on the left. When opposite Rookery Farm, turn left over an old bridge and immediately turn right to join the farm drive, which leads out past white gateposts to a road. Keep straight on along the road.

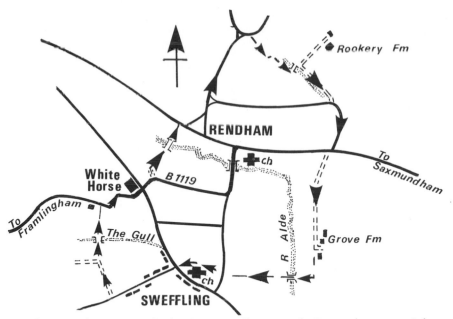

In ¼ mile you reach the Saxmundham road. Cross almost straight over to take the wide track towards Grove Farm. Pass on the left a white house called Lady Whincups, where the poet George Crabbe lived. In ¼ mile, after passing the magnificent three-storey pargeted farmhouse, reach the barns of Grove Farm. Where the concrete farm road ends and a tractor track swings to the left towards some round silos, go straight on through a gate facing you, into a meadow. Continue with the field boundary on the left. There is a transformer on a pole about 20 yards beyond the gate.

At the next field division, there is a stile in the hedge on the left. Here turn right to cross the river Alde by a long footbridge. Walk away from the river with a hedge and ditch on the right. As you approach the corner of the field, go over a stile and walk for 20 yards between a fence and a hedge to the corner of the field. Turn left and walk beside a wood for a few yards. Here turn right and enter the wood.

The narrow footpath through the trees continues through a newer plantation into a large field. Cross the field, keeping parallel to the hedge on the right, and you will pass a shallow pit on the right. From this point, walk straight across a field which has been sown with meadow grasses under the Countryside Premium Scheme, and out to the road.

Cross the road and go straight up the lane, passing Sweffling rectory, to the church. Keep the churchyard to your left and, when you come to a metal gate in front of you, turn right and then left into a narrow way between a brick garden wall and a wire fence, which leads to the road at Sweffling.

Go straight over, along the road opposite the footpath you have been following, and, at the corner, pass a converted barn on the right. You will come, on the right, to another field planted under the Countryside Premium Scheme. A little further on pass a row of houses on the left. In about 50 yards, go right on a grassy lane with a hedge on the right. Here is the third Countryside Premium field.

At the corner of the field the track bends left into a green lane. Here go almost straight on with a large hedge on the left. Bear away slightly from the hedge towards a narrow gap in the far hedge about 50 yards from the field corner and in line with an electricity pole. Find the gap and go down over a sleeper bridge and up the other side and follow a hedge on the left up the hill to a road. Turn right along the road round a double bend. At the road junction follow the main road round to the left and down the hill to return to the White Horse.

Ramsholt
The Ramsholt Arms

Ramsholt is in a remote part of the Deben estuary. It is a very small, isolated place on the east side of the river, beloved of sailors, bird-watchers and those who love the solitude of the river margins.

The inn was originally a ferryman's cottage in the early 18th century. Later it was a shooting lodge and in 1912 it changed to become an alehouse. It is in a spectacular position overlooking the river, with large windows giving panoramic views. Yachts move up and down the river all summer, and often there are magnificent sunsets to be seen. On the bar walls are old photos of Ramsholt. When days get chilly a blazing log fire burns in the large grate. There is a paved terrace for summer meals and drinks.

The pub has a wide repertoire of dishes, including many vegetarian options. Try fresh salmon in light filo pastry, followed by roast pheasant with red wine gravy and bread sauce, and then choose from a wide range of sweets. There is local game in winter and fresh local fish all the year round, such as salmon, skate, cod and mussels. In summer a well-stocked cold buffet table is on offer as are afternoon teas with scones, cream and strawberries. Real ales include Adnams, Speckled Hen and other local brews. There is a children's menu, and of course soft drinks. Dogs are not welcome inside the pub.

The inn is open all day from spring till autumn, and from 11 am till 3 pm and from 7 pm till 11 pm in winter, except on Sundays when the hours are 12 noon till 3 pm and 7 pm till 10.30 pm.

Telephone: 0394 411229.

How to get there: Ramsholt is about 8 miles south of Woodbridge on the east side of the Deben estuary. Leave the A12 near Woodbridge and take the A1152 to Melton. At a roundabout follow the B1083 for Bawdsey and ½ mile after Shottisham turn right (signed for Ramsholt). In another 1½ miles turn right into Dock Road. At the end of the road, just before the white gates, park in the car park on the left. The Ramsholt Arms is 150 yards down the hill at the water's edge.

Parking: There is a large public car park on the bluff above the pub.

Length of the walk: 2½ miles. Map: OS Landranger 169 Ipswich and The Naze area (GR 308415).

This leisurely walk starts at the water's edge by the quay, and shortly climbs to Ramsholt church, prominent on the hill overlooking the river. The route skirts round and later crosses this hill, from where there are wide views of the Deben, stretching up to Woodbridge in the distance.

To appreciate this area fully you need several visits, at various times of year. It is unfrequented and silent in winter, the haunt of many wildfowl and wading birds, and the peaceful river has a unique attraction. In summer there is a marked contrast. The river is a paradise for sailors and small craft are plying up and down between anchorages upstream and the sea. With 200 moorings nearby, the area can at times be a hive of activity. Many birds are still there, but the winter migrants have left and the shyer birds keep well away from the boating activity.

The Walk

Leave the pub and go north along the shore. In 200 yards, when the woods on the right end, leave the riverbank, going down right and through a metal wicket gate. Follow the wandering path over the grazing marsh, curving round to the right at the far side to leave by a metal farm gate which leads into a sandy track. Ten yards after the gate, where the track divides, take the right fork and climb up a sunken lane to the church. At the junction at the top, turn left on a broad, sandy farm track, parallel to the river on your left.

From the high point on this track you can see to the right, across the point, a part of the river upstream towards Waldringfield. Away to the left across the river is Kirton Creek, and half-left is the brick tower of Hemley church.

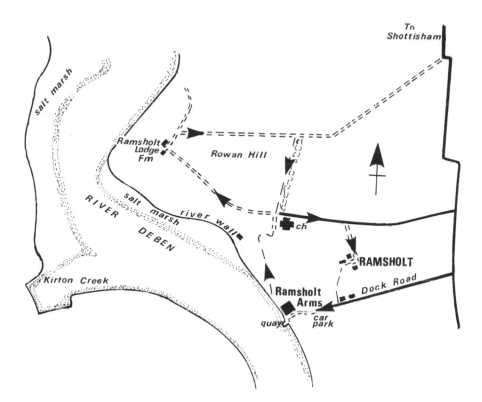

As you get nearer to Ramsholt Lodge Farm you will be walking through an avenue of lime trees. See the characteristic fuzz of young red shoots at the base of these limes.

At the farm buildings turn right, passing brick Cliff Cottage, 1904, on your left. At the next junction go right, rising slightly with the hedge on the right. Away left is a fine view of Waldringfield and Woodbridge, seen through a scant row of pines. Pass a track off to the left and keep straight on, with the hedge on the left. At the next cross-hedge turn right and walk with the tall, wide hedge on the left, down to the church again.

Turn left on a sandy road, with an open field on the left and a few pines on the right. Pass an old stubby cross-hedge on the left and in 100 yards turn right on a track that goes to Ramsholt old school. With the hedge on the left, drop down, curving round to the right and passing the old school on the right, and cottages on the left. After

101

passing another cottage on the right, take the track to the left that goes downhill, curving to the left. Climb quite steeply up a sunken lane and out to join the road. There is a good view of Felixstowe, and beyond to ships at sea approaching the Haven Ports.

Turn right along the road and walk back to the car park.

Butley lies between Rendlesham Forest and Tunstall Forest, on the Butley river. Both forests were devastated in the great storm of 1987, but now thousands of young trees are slowly growing on the cleared land. The soil in the area is light and sandy – excellent for carrots, which are harvested here by the ton.

The fascinating Butley Oyster is many hundreds of years old, built at a time when oysters were commonplace rather than a delicacy as they are now. The smugglers who once frequented the inn probably came up Butley Creek, which is now better known as the source of the crabs, lobsters and oysters cooked here. The pub, which, prior to 1988, was managed by just one family for 72 years, is a traditional 'local'. Every Sunday evening there is a Folk Night, held here for going on 70 years, and the pub fields a winning team in local village quoits, played with large steel rings. There is play equipment in the garden and barbecues are held in summer and in winter. Don't miss the two mounting blocks, still to be seen outside.

On the menu are such dishes as oyster seafood platter, crab au gratin, served hot with salad and new potatoes, lobster dishes, home-made game pie with port wine sauce and salmon quiche. Giant Ma

Barry's Yorkshire pudding filled with mince and mash is something to contend with on a raw winter's day. No meals are available on Mondays. Real ales are Adnams Broadside, Bitter and Mild. Beamish and Guinness are also served and Scrumpy draught cider is on tap. The pub is open all day on Saturdays. Dogs on leads are welcome.
Telephone: 0394 450790.

How to get there: Butley is on the Woodbridge to Orford road. From the A12 at the northern end of the Woodbridge bypass take the A1152 towards Melton. After crossing the river Deben take the left fork, still the A1152, and at the next junction take the B1084 towards Orford.

Parking: There is parking behind the inn and also a little in the front.

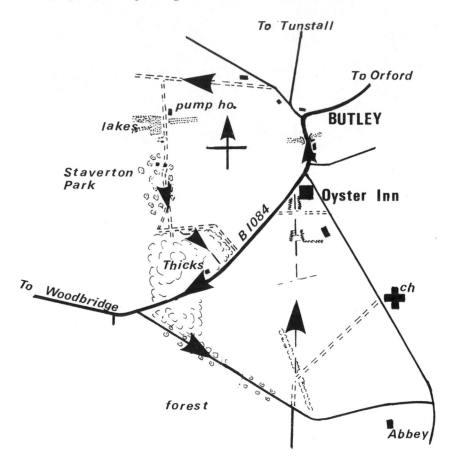

Length of the walk: 4 miles. Map: OS Landranger 156 Saxmundham, Aldeburgh and surrounding area (GR 368509).

From the village, after following the shallow valley of the upper reaches of the Butley river, the walk passes the margin of a large man-made lake, which has attracted a colony of ducks and geese. A sandy track then leads through Staverton Park, past many ancient gnarled oaks. This is a medieval deer park, over 450 years old. In those times, fallow deer were reared in deer parks as food for the wealthy. It is interesting to see that today deer farming has returned to Staverton Park. It was here that Eric Hosking, the eminent bird photographer, spent hour upon hour when a boy, in the company of the estate gamekeeper, learning to lie low, watching the wildlife.

The walk continues through Staverton Thicks, an ancient and atmospheric area of woodland where wild deer, both fallow and muntjac, roam. It then returns across light sandy fields to Butley.

The Walk

From the front of the pub walk along The Street, up to the T-junction and turn left into Wantisden, towards Tunstall and Snape. In 200 yards, at the next junction, keep left along the 'no through road'. After 150 yards bear left off the road on a grassy track. Follow this sandy track under three electricity wires on wooden poles, for almost ¾ mile. Keep on the track which swings left and goes towards a small brick pumphouse. Pass the pumphouse, left, and then a lake on the right, dug out alongside the river to provide a reservoir serving the irrigation system of the area's dry sandy farmland. At a Y-junction, by the area where the farmed deer are enclosed and you can see 6 ft high deer-fencing, keep left and start to climb the hill.

In the valley to your left are thousands of daffodils, and on the hillside above it is a carpet of bluebells, each in their season. Away up on the right, half-hidden, is a flint-faced, thatched keeper's cottage. As you go up the track you have Staverton Park on your right. When the path again divides take the left fork, keeping parallel with the edge of a vast field 50 yards away to your left.

Soon you reach a four-way junction of tracks in a small clearing. Here go left for 20 yards, and, when opposite on your left a gap leading to the corner of the field, go right on a narrow path into Staverton Thicks. This part of the forest is very old and has scarcely been touched by man for centuries. Some of the tall hollies are thought to have been growing for over 400 years.

At first the path is roughly parallel with the farm track, but later it swings right, deeper into the Thicks. Eventually you emerge from the woodland and leave by a gap in a post-and-rail fence to join a road. Butley church is ahead in the distance.

Turn right along the road, passing another flint and thatch keeper's cottage, with church-style windows. Follow, with care, the road as far as a T-junction to the left, where you go left towards Butley Low Corner and Butley High Corner.

Walk along this very pleasant lane, where there are clumps of beech trees at intervals, until you reach a T-junction. Turn left here on to a broad, sandy track, opposite the road which leads to Capel St Andrew. When it goes half-right, you go straight on and quite soon meet a fir shelter belt, at an angle. After 15 yards go obliquely right, through it. Go over the stile into a large field. Half-left on the skyline you can see some buildings, including what was once a school. Follow the rolled path over the field towards the left end of all those buildings, walking at roughly 30 degrees to the shelter belt.

Deviating not a whit, you carry on, due north, to the corner of the onetime school playing field, then on with a chainlink fence on your right. Pass through a gap between a pair of metal gates, on across the next field to another pair of gates, and out by a gap to a cross-track.

Go straight ahead into a delightful green lane. Towards the end you pass beside a clapboard building on a brick base, and so round to the front of the Oyster Inn, with a dovecote against the north wall.

26 Hulver
The Hulvergate Lodge

Hulver is just a few miles south of the river Waveney and the Suffolk border with Norfolk. It lies between Beccles and Lowestoft.

The Hulvergate Lodge is about 400 years old. It has been a pub for many years and for one 150-year period up to recent times it was in the care of just one family. Inside there are many settles, grouped in pairs around small tables, in the spacious, comfortable bar area. The restaurant looks out over a large patio to mown lawns, with a lake beyond. There are aviaries in the seven-acre grounds. Children are welcome in the family area of the pub and in the gardens. Dogs, however, are best left off the premises.

The inn specialises in fish dishes. They can be grilled, fried, battered or breaded, and served with either véronique, mornay or bonne femme sauces. Or there is smoked fillet of trout filled with prawns, and salad. A choice of vegetarian dishes, for example, three-bean chilli with rice, and vegetarian Stroganoff is offered, as well as salad, American-style snacks and a children's menu. Delicious home-made soup is served as are such dishes as steak and kidney pie, lasagne, chicken Kiev, chilli con carne and lamb chops. Adnams, Worthington and Bass real ales are available and Dry Blackthorn draught cider.

Telephone: 0507 76254.

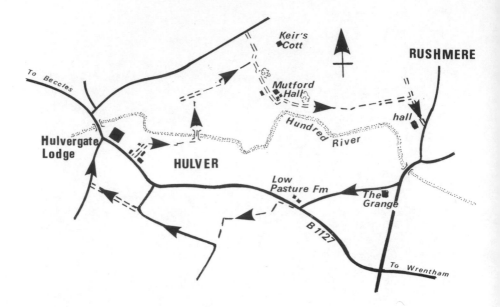

How to get there: The Hulvergate Lodge stands at a road junction at Hulver on the B1127, which runs between Wrentham on the A12 and the A146 east of Beccles.

Parking: A large car park is adjacent to the inn.

Length of the walk: 4½ miles. Map: OS Landranger 156 Saxmundham, Aldeburgh and surrounding area (GR 466872).

The walk takes you around the shallow valley of the Hundred river, which formed the boundary between the Blything Hundred and the Mutford and Lothingland Hundred, when in Saxon times the country was divided for administrative purposes into Hundreds (comprising roughly 100 families or farm holdings). The tiny river meanders for about 10 miles from Ellough, near Beccles, to the sea at Kessingland.

Good field edge and cross-field paths, and green lanes, make easy walking, while interesting old houses, many with crow-stepped gables, are often to be seen.

The Walk

From the Hulvergate Lodge, go left along the road, climbing gently. At the crest go left off the road into Sandy Lane. Follow the wide track, passing a few houses on the right, then, when the track swings right, go straight ahead between hedges, past a house on the left and turn right along a headland path, with the hedge on the left.

Ignore the tempting stile on the left and continue, still with the hedge on the left, to the point where the hedge makes a slight turn to the right. Here go half-left through the hedge over an iron hurdle. Look ahead. There is a thicket a little to the right, and in the next hedge-line, right of a small, distant, brick building, is a large oak. Go to it.

Beside the tree, cross the footbridge and then cross the fence. Head across the field, slightly to the right of the brick building, and go over a footbridge over the Hundred river. Go to the far right corner of this long, narrow field and leave by a grey metal gate. A very short, fenced area leads into a small field. Walk to the far left corner, to another grey metal gate which takes you into a green lane. Turn right.

When the lane ends, in 100 yards, pass a hurdle and cross a culvert. Continue in roughly the same direction, to the hedge on the far side of the field. Here turn left along the headland to the corner of the field, where you turn right through the hedge into a huge field. Continue in much the same direction on the rolled path over this field, climbing slightly to the crest. You now have wide views in all directions. You can see half-left the round-towered Mutford church. At the far side of this field join a tarmac track, near a bend on the left. Ahead across the field is Keir's Cottage, with crow-stepped gables.

Turn right along the track, with the hedge on the left. Pass a wood on the left, then some barns on the right. Mutford Hall, with massive chimneys and, again, crow-stepped gables, is on your left.

At the end, keep on the concrete, going round to the left, round the edge of an open barn, with corrugated iron sheeting on your right. Go through a metal gate which unlatches, into a wide track. Pass a cottage with a circular window over its porch. Follow the grassy track as it winds, with a hedge on the left and a barbed wire fence on the right. Pass through a gate, and later come to a gate across the path, with a stile to the left of it, close to a wooded dell.

Go over the stile and on with a barbed wire fence on your left. The land falls away on the right, down to New Cut. The fence you will follow is at the edge of the plateau on the left. Later, go over a stile and on, then over a stile in a metal hurdle, into a narrow but very long field. Go left on the field edge path, with a barbed wire fence on the left, the field getting narrower as you go. Leave the field by a metal gate and continue along a farm track, with the hedge on the left. Half-right is Rushmere Hall. Pass through a metal gate and you now have hedges both sides. Meet another track at right angles, go right and walk out past Rushmere Hall with its pedimented windows and, again, crow-stepped gables, to the road.

At the road turn right, walk to the T-junction and go right, towards Wrentham and Ipswich. Pass the village sign, with its imagery of

Rushmere, and continue till, after crossing the Hundred river again, you reach a byway to the right. This is Tinkers Lane.

Walk the whole length of this quiet, narrow road. At the end go right a few yards to the farm entrance of Low Pasture Farm, then go up into the field on the left and follow the footpath sign along its side. Turn left along a wide, grassy cart track with the hedge and fence on the right. At an internal field corner go right, still following the fence on the right. The track is now a narrow bridlepath. Then enter a 10 ft wide area where there are tree stumps and young trees.

At the top of the hill there are good views to the right, over to Mutford Hall which you passed earlier. At a stockade of old sleepers, turn left and follow a grassy cart track across the field. Leave the field by a red metal farm gate to meet a road at a bend. Turn right and walk along the road. Descend a slight hill, with pine woods on the right. When the road makes a sharp right turn, go straight ahead on a green lane, with hedges on both sides.

Come out on a road and walk right, downhill, to the T-junction and your start at the Hulvergate Lodge.

Blythburgh
The White Hart

Anyone travelling up the coast road, the A12, to Lowestoft will beome aware of Blythburgh church dominating the crossing of the Blyth river valley. Holy Trinity church, standing on high ground above the river, dominates the low-lying marshes and reed beds of the estuary downstream, and the wide valley upstream. It is even more dramatic when floodlit at night. Further east the river widens out greatly in the marshland, before running out to sea between Southwold and Walberswick. At one time Blythburgh was a thriving town and port, with boats plying up the river between Southwold harbour and Halesworth. In the 15th century the river was navigable up to Halesworth, yes, navigable but shallow, and as bigger, deeper-draught ships became customary so the river was used less and less, and trade declined.

The busy White Hart inn was built, it is believed, in the 11th century and was the old court house in times past. Customers in the single large lounge are warmed, on cold days, by two wood fires. One is conventionally placed at the end of the room, but the other is a very big fire on a free-standing open hearth. The smoke is drawn up through a huge conical cowl. Brass ornaments abound, including, by the hearth, a boot jack in the form of a grasshopper. Both hot and cold food can be ordered at the salad bar at the far end, where a range of salads, cold pies and quiches is displayed. Hot dishes include Suffolk chicken pie, fresh locally caught cod or plaice, chicken nuggets with a spicy dip, Blythburgh fish pie, a three-egg omelette with a choice of fillings, and half a pound of sausages and chips, just to name a few. Adnams real ales are on offer, as are Strongbow and Woodpecker cider. There is a beer garden and a play area for children. Well-behaved dogs on leads are welcome.

Telephone: 050 270217.

How to get there: Blythburgh is about 10 miles south-west of Lowestoft on the A12, and the White Hart stands on the main road near the bridge.

Parking: It is suggested that you do not leave your car in the pub's car park when out walking, as it is a very busy pub and the car park fills up with customers. There is a large car park close to the church.

Length of the walk: 4 miles. Map: OS Landranger 156 Saxmundham, Aldeburgh and surrounding area (GR 453754).

The walk lies in the valley of the river Blyth. At first it follows the river bank, edged with rushes and other marsh plants, upstream. After passing a hospital, formerly the Bulcamp workhouse built in 1765, the route leaves the river and turns across marshy meadows towards Wenhaston. It takes, for a short distance, the route of the former light railway which ran between Halesworth and Southwold. Although opened in 1879 and closed as early as 1929, there are still traces of it remaining.

Blythburgh is a busy village, yet the area covered by this walk is very quiet and isolated.

The Walk
From the White Hart, cross over and walk left along the main road for a few yards, turning right down the first narrow road on your right. After passing an old house called The Priory, which has an old, flint, chapel-like building at one end, and then a half-timbered, thatched-roofed house, you reach the church by a tiny green. This is a large, light and airy building, built mainly in the 15th century, but the tower is much older. Before 1577 there was also a spire, but that crashed through the roof when struck by lightning, killing two people. The expressions on the faces of the carved stone corbels high in the church are worth studying. They are so fresh looking they seem as though they were only recently carved.

At the far right of the green go down a green lane for about 50 yards

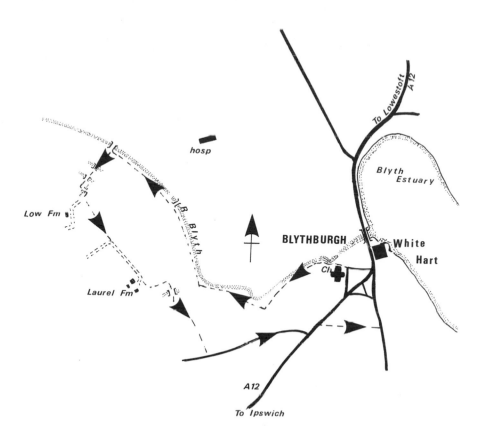

to meet the river. Turn left and follow the river on your right for a long way. At one point you will make a sharp right-hand bend, when you head directly towards the sandhill on the opposite shore. About here the Blythburgh hospital, topped with a white lantern, comes into view from behind the hill on the other side of the river. Continue with the river on the right and a ditch on the left. Sometimes the river is screened from view by the reeds.

Go over one stile, then two close together by a concrete bridge. Keep straight on. Presently you reach a steel bridge with brick abutments and metal handrails. This is the point where you leave the river.

Turn left and walk to the corner and go over the stile into a meadow. Follow the track, with a barbed wire fence on the right. Blyford church is seen far away on your right. Go over a wooden slatted footbridge, and continue with a fence on your left.

Walk over a two-plank footbridge and go on, still with the hedge on the left. When three-quarters of the way along this field you will find a stile and two-plank footbridge on your left. Go across the adjacent field half-right to the diagonal corner of this field, where you will find a stile beside a metal gate under an oak tree.

At this point do not go over the stile – that is a public footpath into Wenhaston village – but go left along a permissive footpath. Carry on along the wide, grass cart track, with fences each side. This is the course of the old railway.

The track ends where a hedge begins on the right. Here, go through a farm gate on to a wide, grass footpath which leads to an avenue of oaks. At the end go right, through a farm gate, to join a track, which has come down the hill, at a bend. Go left along the track, later going through a wide gate, and passing some farm buildings on the right. When the track swings right towards the farm you go almost straight ahead, between post-and-rail fences. The path curves left and widens out. Go over the stile beside the leftmost gate.

Keep on the track, with a ditch on the right, heading for Blythburgh church. Swing right over a wide cart bridge, then left through a gap where there is a stile. From this gap look half-left across the field and you will see another stile under a big oak. Go to that stile, and cross it. You are now near the corner of a big meadow. Look across this, and other fields, to a dark mass of trees. In line with the right of those trees you will see a gap, and in that gap you will see a stile, diagonally across the field. Go to it. From the stile head in the same general direction as before and look for a gap in the far hedge, with a road to be seen behind it. Head for that gap and walk out to the road, Wenhaston Lane.

Turn left and walk along the road to its junction with the A12. Turn left and walk beside the A12 for a few yards, then cross over and turn right down a green track, just before the first house on the right. The track diminishes in width to a path between hedges. When you meet the road go left, and at the next junction bear right and walk straight on towards the White Hart.

28 **Aldringham**
The Parrot and Punchbowl

Aldringham is in the area of Suffolk known as the Sandlings, the broad coastal strip with small pockets of sandy, heathy habitat where heather, grass, gorse and bracken predominate. Birch and pine trees, once kept in check by grazing sheep and rabbits, are now creeping back to the open heath. Two miles away, on the coast, stands Thorpeness, built early this century as a holiday village by a Mr Ogilvie, who also created Thorpe Meare. The Meare, which was dug out of a former marsh and opened for recreation in 1912, is a haunt of duck and grebe and where, in summer, young and old may float around in hired craft. It is dotted with small islands which children find fascinating to land on and explore.

The Parrot and Punchbowl is one of the oldest pubs in Suffolk, dating back at least to 1591. It is an attractive hostelry with seating areas on three different levels. Music plays at a soothing volume. The food is good and much of it is home-made, including soup, lasagne verdi, chilli con carne and chicken curry. There is fresh fish from the griddle, salmon cutlets, cod and plaice fillets. Suffolk Smokies, which are pieces of smoked haddock in a creamy sauce, are served with brown toast and butter. Real ales such as Whitbread,

Flowers and Adnams are available, and Strongbow cider. There is a garden area for children, and well-behaved dogs on leads are welcome.

Telephone: 0728 830221.

How to get there: Aldringham is a small village between Leiston and Aldeburgh. From the south, take the A12 towards Lowestoft. Just after Farnham, follow the A1094 towards Aldeburgh for 3½ miles, then turn off on to the B1069 (signed 'Leiston'). In 2 miles, go right for Thorpeness. Aldringham is reached in ½ mile. From the north go to Yoxford on the A12, and from the west take the A1120 Stowmarket to Yoxford road. At Yoxford, take the B1122 through Leiston and on towards Aldeburgh. In a mile, at a crossroads, you reach the Parrot and Punchbowl.

Parking: There is a car park behind the pub.

Length of the walk: 5½ miles. Map: OS Landranger 156 Saxmundham, Aldeburgh and surrounding area (GR 447610).

Passing the isolated Aldringham church with the terrace of the Ogilvie Almshouses alongside, the walk crosses sandy fields and descends to the margin of Thorpe Meare. The way passes between the 'House in the Clouds' and the restored Thorpeness Windmill, now the Heritage Coast Centre, to Thorpeness, where, if time permits, you can go out to the beach and the North Sea.

The route then crosses Aldringham Heath, where birch, gorse, oak and heather are abundant.

The Walk

From the Parrot and Punchbowl cross the road and go 200 yards along the B1122 road towards Aldeburgh. Bear left along a gravel track, passing a pale-washed bungalow on the right. When the track swings left to the old school buildings keep straight on over a grassy path between fences, passing the old school on the left.

In about ¼ mile enter a wood and continue straight ahead. You will soon reach a path junction, where a small metal gate leads into a churchyard. Here turn left and climb a sunken lane to reach the church car park and the end of a tarmac road. Note the long brick terrace of the Ogilvie Almshouses, an attractive building and rather unusual in its isolated setting.

Enter the churchyard, then turn left and walk through it, keeping the boundary on your left. Leave by the iron gate and keep on the footpath with a blackthorn hedge on the left. At a corner of a field go over a V-shaped stile and straight across a field to another similar stile.

116

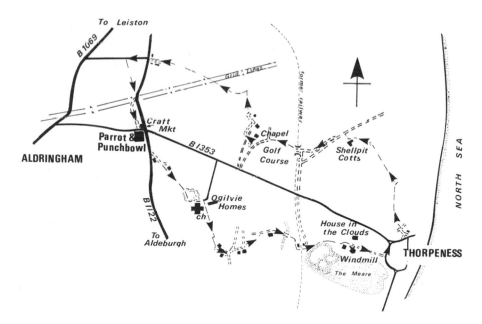

Turn right and follow the edge of the field round to the left, keeping in the same general direction, till at the end of the field you bear left on a cart track. Pass some barns on the left and a bungalow on the right, go up a slight rise and at a junction of three tracks turn left Twenty yards on bear right at the next junction of tracks, to pass two dwellings. Near the second, a chalet bungalow, the track bends left. Just after the bend turn right, off the cart track and onto a narrow footpath through uncultivated heathland, birch, oaks, brambles and gorse. In a few yards cross a cart track and continue on the narrow footpath.

You will come out to another sandy cart track where you turn right, as the sign indicates, to pass an isolated pair of houses on the right. The building is decoratively faced with pebbles of very uniform size, no doubt using local materials. You will see similar decoration again later on this walk.

The track ends at the houses but keep straight on along a well-used grass footpath. Cross a marshy area by a timber boardwalk and, shortly after, bear half-right following a sign, to reach a former level crossing of the railway which once ran to Aldeburgh. You can still see the remains of the gates and the substantial railway gateposts. On the left is a bungalow descriptively called Crossing Cottage. Cross the line and pass Mere Cottage on the left.

At this point there is the option of a short cut. Anyone not wanting to visit Thorpeness can turn left alongside Mere Cottage and go northward on the track parallel to the former railway. Cross the B1353 and keep straight on until the track comes to the brick abutments of a onetime railway bridge, to rejoin the circular walk.

Continuing the main walk, having passed Mere Cottage keep straight on along a narrow path. In about 50 yards follow on the right a narrow stretch of water, being part of Thorpe Meare. Keep on the grass path skirting the Meare with the golf course on the left. Climb, past the club house on the right, to reach a tarmac road. Pass the restored windmill on the right, and, on the left, the House in the Clouds. These two buildings were linked by a common purpose in the 1920s. The windmill pumped water from a well into a water tank for the village water supply. The tank, disguised as a house, sits at the top of a tower comprising a five-storey dwelling.

When you reach the road in the centre of Thorpeness turn left. In 200 yards keep right at the grass triangle and pass the Dolphin Inn. Turn left opposite a lane called The Sanctuary on a gravel road for about 30 yards and continue along a brick rubble track as it swings left at a byway sign.

At a three-way junction, turn right for about 10 yards and then turn left at the corner of a back garden fence onto a broad grass path which leads through an area of gorse and blackberry. You are following the edge of the heathland with a hawthorn hedge on the left and, ahead, the massive cubical structure of Sizewell Generating Station a few miles away.

Eventually you reach the end of the heathland, where the track you have been following veers to the right. Here leave the well-worn track and go slightly left on a narrow sunken grass path. In ¼ mile, where the field on the right gives way to a wood, bear left, keeping on a grass track through an area of bracken with small silver birch trees, in the direction slightly to the right of a building known as Shellpit Cottages, seen in the distance. It is a large house with pebbles embedded in the walls.

Turn right at the house, still on a grass track. Shortly, reach a major path at right angles. Turn left on to the well-used track. Where the track splits into two apparently parallel paths, take the right-hand one which gradually swings away round to the right. This leads to the embankment of the disused railway where the path runs between the abutment walls of a former bridge. The short cut, mentioned earlier, rejoins the route here.

Beyond the bridge keep straight on, following a grass path over the golf course, taking care as you cross several fairways. At the far side, join a sandy track at a bend and continue straight on. Come to an isolated building on the right, the former Providence Baptist Chapel (1812 and 1915). Turn right on a narrow path between sections of the churchyard and then turn right and left, following a sandy cart track.

Cross straight over a tarmac drive to Stone House and immediately turn right, still on a cart track, with woods on the right and a fence on the left. Pass the house and make a sharp turn to the left by a high brick wall. Leave the track where it turns right and go straight on along a headland path with a hedge on the right. At the next field boundary turn left and follow the hedge on the left. Go under the grid lines and, still keeping the hedge on the left, walk out to the Leiston–Aldeburgh road.

Cross straight over and go down Goldings Lane. Pass new Ogilvie Homes on the left and then about 10 yards beyond a cul-de-sac on the right, go left on a well-used field path. On the far side of the field join a lane and turn right. The lane leads to the Aldringham Craft Market, the Parrot and Punchbowl and your start.

Other local attractions: Thorpeness, passed on the walk, merits a return visit for boating on the Meare, and for the quiet enjoyment of the lonely sea and the sky, on the shingly beach, which is only yards from the Meare. The Aldringham Craft Market, just opposite the Parrot and Punchbowl, is well worth a visit. Its outward appearance belies the large treasure chest of interesting craft ideas, toys, books, carvings, paintings, garden pots, jams etc for sale. It is open all year round, Monday to Saturday 10 am to 5.30 pm; Sundays from the end of September till Easter 2 pm to 5.30 pm, from Easter till end September 10 am to 12 noon and 2 pm to 5.30 pm.

29 Lound
The Village Maid

Lound, in the far north-east of the county, has a quite remarkable church. It is called, with reason, the 'Golden Church'. From the outside, in spite of its round tower, it seems very ordinary, but the inside, even on a dark winter's day with no artificial illumination save the sanctuary lamp, seems ablaze with light and colour. In the village a tale is told of highwaymen robbing a coach near the village, which was on a main coaching route. All but one of the highwaymen escaped, but the one who was caught had carried the loot, which he had thrown into the village pond. On his death-bed he is said to have confessed to the vicar, who had the large pond dredged and the gold and jewels were recovered. And that, the story says, was the source of the wealth by which the church was decorated. However the church guide leaflet says nothing of that!

In the middle of the village is the pub, built around 1800, on the site of an earlier coaching house. The drinking and eating area extends right across the full width of the pub and there are views across the large village pond (or mardle, as they call it in these parts), and the ducks and geese are very friendly, walking across the road to see what is going on at the pub. Low walls subdivide the pub into small intimate areas. All the food served is fresh and home-cooked, chosen from a continuously changing menu. For instance, there is smoked salmon, rump steak and all the trimmings, leek and Stilton bake, cidery apple crumble and treacle sponge pudding. At this freehouse you can drink Greene King, Tetley, Burton and Tolly ales or Taunton Dry Blackthorn cider. There is a garden area for children and dogs are permitted in the public bar.

Telephone: 0502 730441.

How to get there: Lound is about 5 miles north-west of Lowestoft, and midway between the A12 and A143 (Bungay–Great Yarmouth road). It is 1½ miles north of Blundeston on the B1074. The Village Maid is in the centre of the village by the pond.

Parking: There is a car park behind the pub, and there is also a car park on the opposite side of the road by the pond.

Length of the walk: 6 miles. Map: OS Landranger 134 Norwich and the Broads (GR 505992).

Although quite long, the walk is easy. At first it follows a country lane to the small, well cared-for thatched church of St Mary Ashby, standing remote in a field. It then visits the village of Somerleyton, with the school and many delightful estate cottages surrounding the spacious green. Then there is a stretch on the Angles Way, a route running from Great Yarmouth along the Waveney valley to Knettishall Heath, where it joins the end of the Peddars Way and the Icknield Way.

The walk then follows the side of a small slope which forms the edge of the Somerleyton marshes, through which the river Waveney runs to Breydon Water and out to the sea at Great Yarmouth.

The Walk

Take the lane, known as Snake's Lane, beside the Village Maid, which soon leads into a large field. Keep on in the same direction on a well-used cart track, first with a hedge on the left, then on the right. In about a mile, where the main track swings right at a T-junction, go left along another cart track leading to 13th century Ashby church. The Norman base of the tower is round, but surmounted by an octagonal upper part. Note the brick quoins up the tower angles.

Go straight on past the church, keeping the well-trimmed hedge on the left, and in ½ mile cross, at right angles, a lane leading to Kitty's Farm on the left. Continue with the hedge on the left to meet the tarmac drive to Somerleyton Hall. Turn right and walk out past iron gates, and a thatched gatehouse on the right, to the road.

Turn left along the road, following the brick perimeter wall of

121

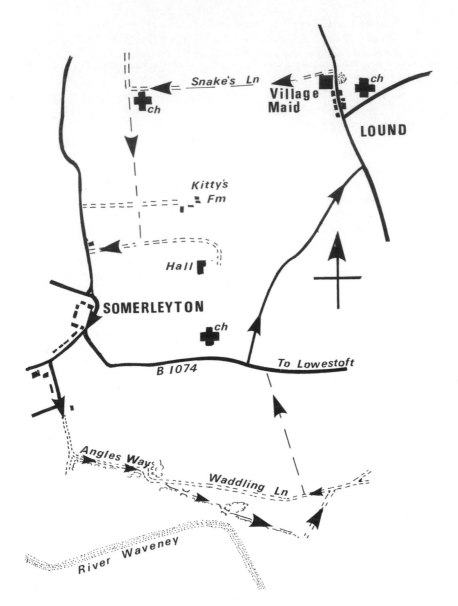

Somerleyton Park. At the T-junction keep left and walk past the school to the wide village green, with charming cottages on three sides, built for his workers by Sir Samuel Peto, one of the great Victorian railway builders, who lived at the Hall around 1850.

At the green the main road swings sharply left. Here go straight on – there are houses away to the right. In 300 yards pass, on the left, a footpath leading to the church, and in another 100 yards turn left into Station Road and walk along it. After the last houses on the right the road makes a sharp right turn. Here, by the entrance to Waveney Grange Farm, go straight on along a rutted cart track between hedges. You have now joined the Angles Way.

In 300 yards, at the fork, take the left path, with woods on the right. You can see between the trees the Waveney valley to the right. Descend a little and join a track coming in from the left. In about 200 yards Waddling Lane, the track you have been following, starts to rise, with woods on the left. Here go half-right through a kissing-gate on to a pleasant, grassy footpath. Soon you reach a short boardwalk, and after that you follow the edge of the wood on the right, where there is a good view of the Waveney.

At the waymark turn sharp right into the woods, down across a wet area by a boardwalk, and up the other side. Follow a field boundary for a further ¼ mile and then go over a stile into a sandy lane. Turn left. The lane rises to join Waddling Lane at right angles, where you turn left. At the first cross-hedge on the right, go right through a narrow gate into a field, and continue, following the hedge on the right. Go through gaps in two cross-hedges and, still following the hedge on the right, go over a stile and out to the road.

Turn left on the road and take the first road to the right, called Green Lane, to Lound. After a mile reach a T-junction. Turn left and return to your start at the Village Maid, ½ mile along the road.

Take time, if you can, to visit the fascinating church. As you enter by the south porch the height of the font cover, its brilliant colour and the colours of the roof beam above it, present an amazing sight. Then jettied out from the west end, above the nave, is a glittering organ case with its many golden pipes. Looking towards the east end is a richly carved and decorated rood screen, and beyond that the high altar with its gilded bronze angels. Through the thickness of the west wall is an unusual squint, a cylindrical hole whereby the altar can be seen from the churchyard. On the north wall is a modern wall painting of St Christopher, and included in it is a motorcar and an aeroplane.

Other local attractions: Somerleyton Hall and gardens, with the famous yew maze, set in 3,000 acres of parkland, are open to the public three or four days a week from Easter till late September. No dogs are allowed. Telephone 0502 732143 to check opening times.

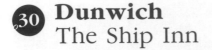

Dunwich
The Ship Inn

Picturesque Dunwich is a popular place all year round and even on a dry and windy day in mid-winter there will be many visitors. It traces its history back to medieval times, when it was a flourishing port with a sheltered harbour and a thriving trade with the rest of East Anglia and with the Continent. Over the centuries the sea has destroyed so much. Around 1250, because of storms, the harbour entrance became blocked with shingle, and so trade was lost to other ports along the coast. Also the sea has relentlessly claimed the cliffs and the land. Over ¼ mile has gone in the last 50 years, and in 1992 alone a total of 5 yards was lost to the sea in storms.

The Ship Inn is an old smugglers' inn. It has a welcoming atmosphere, with many eating areas, both inside and out, as well as the restaurant. In the Ship Bar you may, if you wish, sit on an upholstered barrel. There is a large garden behind the pub, with an old fig tree. Children will be happy playing here. The food, served from The Galley, is varied and excellent. Not surprisingly, fish, much of it locally caught fresh fish, is a popular item on the menu here, for instance the Ship's seafood pancakes, Dunwich deep-fried plaice, hot prawns oozing with garlic butter, prawn ploughman's and poached salmon

124

steaks cooked in white wine. This is not to say that other tastes are not catered for. There is chicken vol-au-vent, rump steak, pork escalope stuffed full of ham and cheese, and a variety of puddings. The Ship is a freehouse serving ales from two local brewers, Greene King and Adnams. Adnams Broadside is featured in summer and Adnams Old in winter. Strongbow draught cider is on offer too. The Ship has overnight accommodation. Well-behaved dogs on leads are welcome.

Telephone: 072 873219.

How to get there: Dunwich is an isolated coastal village just 4 miles, as the crow flies, from Southwold, but there is no direct route. From the A12 at Blythburgh, take the B1125 (Westleton) road and in 2 miles turn left. Alternatively, from Darsham on the A12, take the minor road to Westleton and then go through the village, bearing right for Dunwich. The Ship Inn is on the village street close to the shore.

Parking: The Ship Inn has a very small car park but nearby there is a large, well-signed, public car park close to the shore.

Length of the walk: The full walk is 5½ miles, but it can be easily shortened to 3 miles. Map: OS Landranger 156 Saxmundham, Aldeburgh and surrounding area (GR 477706).

This figure-of-eight walk from the Ship Inn goes down the village street, where almost every house has decorative carved bargeboards. Possibly Church Farm, a few yards up the road from the church, has the most elaborate of all. Passing St James's church the walk goes inland to cross Dunwich Heath, a sandy heather-covered area, to reach the soft cliffs overlooking the sea near the former coastguard cottages. It returns over the heath, through mixed woodland and then on the coast path past the ruins of a friary.

The Walk

Turn left from the Ship and walk to the grassy triangle by the church. Go almost straight ahead into the bridleway just to the right of the war memorial. Follow this shingly green lane, with a steep bank 30 yards away to the left, pass a pair of cottages and keep straight on, rising slightly on an earth track now. There are many newer trees, alder, cherry, oaks and beech, alongside this track. When you reach Sandy Lane Farm, turn left in front of its black, metal farm gates and climb up the grassy-middled farm track until you reach the Westleton road.

Cross straight over and walk between high hedges on this wide farm track. Pass Mount Pleasant Farm on the left, and, soon after going under three electricity wires, come to a four-way junction of paths. This is the centre point of the figure-of-eight.

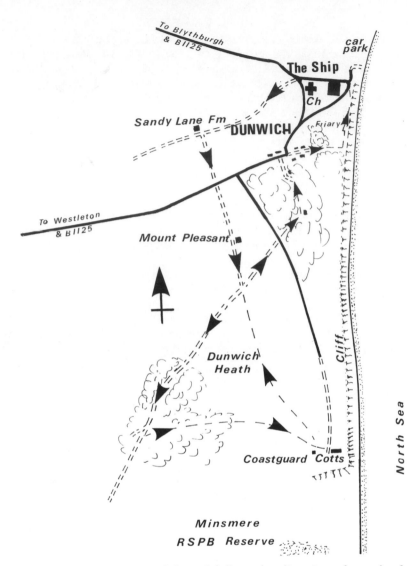

For the shorter walk, turn left and follow the directions from the four-way junction, as for the longer route.

For the longer walk, turn right and go along a wide bridleway, heath on both sides, following at first the electricity supply wires a few yards away on the right. Presently you are in a 10 ft wide cleared track, where the heather scrub has been kept back from the path. After a short rise, see on your left, ½ mile away, the white line of coastguard cottages, stark against the sky.

Enter some mixed woodland — pine and birch — and soon the wide, cleared strip, including the cart track you have been following, veers right through a rustic wooden gate. Your route is straight ahead onto a narrower bridleway. Almost immediately, turn left at the public footpath sign and follow the narrow well-walked path through the mixed woods.

Later the woods end and you cross a stile into National Trust property, Dunwich Heath. Rest on the seat if you will. Climb a short heather-clad hill and at the top again see the coastguard cottages, which are your next objective.

Go to the right of the cottages to see the view from the cliff edge, and then retrace your steps.

By the landward end of the cottages, take the path 'To Eastbridge'. This is the path by which you came, but, soon after the toilet block, swing right and in a few yards leave the path to Eastbridge which swings left, and go straight ahead along a narrow path up over Dunwich Common, waymarked 'Coastal Path'. At the top of the rise there is a seat, with a fine view to the south from this vantage point.

The way is straight on. Now the path widens to an earth cart track. It bends slightly to the right and then curves in a wide arc to the left. Remember that your route is straight across the heath. Therefore, when nearly round the bend in the cart track and at the 'Coast Path' sign, turn right off the cart track onto a narrow heather-girt path.

The heather gives way to bracken and soon the narrow footpath reaches the end of the green lane and the four-way junction where you were earlier on. Turn right on a broad earth track, with grass in the middle.

Both routes continue from here. In 200 yards, at a clearing, see Mount Pleasant Farm away to the left. Go straight ahead along a green lane with high hedges on both sides. Come out on a road, the Minsmere Road, turn right for 10 yards and then left on the public footpath to Dunwich. It is a broad, meandering earth path through woodland.

At a cross-tracks by a white bungalow, cross straight over and continue, curving a little to the right. Presently, curve left and you now have a long, broad, straight path ahead of you, some 20 ft wide through mixed woods with lots of sweet chestnuts and rhododendrons. Pass a cottage and its garages. Do you see the man forever playing golf? Soon, by a wooden farm gate, reach the road.

Turn right to the junction. Do not swing left but carry straight on, along a wide, gravelly track. Further on see, set in the white gates, two white friars, and later on two more. Pass a three-way footpath sign, and Suffolk County Council's Greyfriars Wood. Go ahead under a brick arch with the sea now visible. Go left just before the wooden barrier which reminds you not to fall over the cliff edge, and go left up some steps, following the coast path. In 100 yards turn left, go between two posts and fork right. Climb over the broad, low, ladder stile into the friary precinct. This friary was built in 1289 and replaced an earlier one founded here by the Franciscan order.

By the wooden gate into Dunwich Greyfriars go right a yard or so, then left, rejoining the old cliff-edge path. In 10 yards note one of the last remaining gravestones up here. Where the track soon divides, the right fork takes you to a display board with a dramatic reconstruction of what the view would have been like from here in 1230. All gone beneath the waves.

Rejoin the narrow path and walk down it to meet the road. Go right a little, then left to get back to the Ship.

Other local attractions: On Dunwich Heath, at the coastguard cottages, there is a visitor centre with display boards about the heath, while upstairs is a panoramic window and binoculars for looking up and down the coast and out to sea. There is also a tearoom and a National Trust shop. The Trust lets one or two of the cottages to holidaymakers. What a delightful spot for a holiday.

There is a museum not far from the Ship in St James's Street. It contains a model of Dunwich in the 11th and 12th centuries. There is a wildlife room and a social history room as well as many artefacts from Roman, Saxon and medieval times, and of course there is a souvenir shop. Opening times are March Saturdays and Sundays from 2 pm till 4.30 pm, from Good Friday till the end of September 11.30 am till 4.30 pm daily, and during October from 12 noon till 4 pm daily. Ring 072 87 3796 for more details.

Dunwich is a fine centre for the RSPB reserve at Minsmere, one of the most celebrated in the country, just 15 minutes' walk away.

It is also convenient for concerts at Snape Maltings and at Aldeburgh, both only minutes away by car.